celebrating

PETALUMA

celebrating

PETALUMA

EDITED BY

TERRY SMITH

PUBLISHED BY THE

PETALUMA SESQUICENTENNIAL COMMITTEE

and THE PETALUMA VISITORS PROGRAM

SALES & BOURKE, SUCCESSOR
TO MUST HATCH, LATE 1930'S

Contents

150 Years of Change — and More to Come

BY MAYOR PAMELA TORLIATT

As Mayor of the City of Petaluma and a fourth generation Petaluman, I want to welcome residents and visitors alike to our Sesquicentennial Celebration. Petaluma's 150th Birthday is a time to celebrate our past and welcome our future.

Petaluma has maintained her small town character. It is not something we've created. It is her soul. I believe our residents know what a special place we have here in Northern California. We have come a long way in the last century and a half, and part of what makes us unique is that our residents demand that our history be incorporated into what is new.

So many changes have occurred since Petaluma Boulevard was Highway 101, auto dealerships were located downtown, and the downtown buildings turned their backs to the river. In those days,

we built for cars, not people — and we were a strong critical mass for agriculture. Now, Petaluma Boulevard is our historic main street. We have regained a movie theater downtown in addition to live theater at the Mystic. Our river is now a focal point for pedestrians, river craft and businesses. We continue to maintain our agricultural diversity with Dairymen's Feed and Rivertown. But the redevelopment — or should I say *enhancement* — of our downtown signals the community's support for bringing in the new and preserving the old. The community is now seeing the great success of their investment steered by visionary leaders.

There is more to come with the resurrection of a commuter rail and freight service and the creation of a river trail. Through it all, we continue to value historic preservation, art, music, and being connected with our neighbors. I am looking forward to the challenges that face us. We are a great city. Happy Birthday, Petaluma!

THE PETALUMA QUEEN

THE PETALUMA VALLEY FROM SPRING HILL ROAD

This book is a celebration. While it contains much historical information, it is certainly not meant to be a comprehensive study of Petaluma's past. In fact, a century and a half of history in a city as complex and colorful as Petaluma may be too much for any one book to hold. We on the Petaluma Sesquicentennial Committee hope you'll find in this book the spirit of Petaluma — not only the spirit of our town's past, but also the spirit of its present and future.

Within these covers are the thoughts of more than 20 authors and the images of dozens of talented artists and photographers. Many of the contributors are already well known locally for their published work. Five of them have been chosen as "Good Eggs" for their "eggs-ceptional" efforts in preserving Petaluma's history and promoting its quality of life. Many have lived and worked here for decades. Many more are students in local schools or have just recently graduated. What all of them share is a love for Petaluma. It's been a joy to work with them and I've learned a great deal.

One thing that has become quite clear is that history is not always as precise as I once believed it to be. Much of what we call "history" might actually be better described as "lore." Some is "oral history," passed down through a family or an organization for decades — and we all know how a story can change each time it's passed along. Some history comes from personal memory — and the older we get, the less dependable that might be. Some history comes from handwritten notes in family bibles or on the backs of photographs. Some comes from previously written books that probably relied on even older books. The most reliable history often comes from newspapers of the time. We are lucky to have a newspaper with files dating back to before Petaluma was officially a city, but even newspaper files can be confusing.

Some names are spelled in a variety of ways in historical records. Regarding some events, accounts vary. Errors and omissions are unavoidable. Every effort has been made to avoid misrepresentations and mistakes. Still, you may find "history" in this book that contradicts other sources. You may even find "history" in this book that contradicts other "history" in this book. We hope you'll accept the book for what it is meant to be — not so much indisputable fact as a celebration of the spirit of Petaluma's past, present and future.

Another thing that has become clear in the process of compiling this book is that Petaluma is remarkable in its ability to adapt to the future while preserving the best of the past.

PETALUMANS OF YESTERYEAR IN THE 2006 BUTTER & EGG DAYS PARADE

TERRY SMITH

A century and a half ago, this settlement flourished as a shipping port because of its location. Scows, steamers and barges lined up along Petaluma Creek, loading agricultural products bound for San Francisco and beyond. Eventually, the scows and steamers linked with the railroads. There came a time when the river and the railroads were no longer the best conduits for commerce and Petaluma turned its back on the river for awhile. In recent years, however, the river has reasserted itself as an asset. New development has created places to live, work and play along its banks. The river has become a venue for recreation, festivals and events that draw tourists from around the state, the nation and the world.

When dairy cattle proved more adaptable to the climate than beef cattle, a vibrant dairy industry emerged. More recently, large corporate ranches have threatened Petaluma's smaller family operations. Yet, family dairy farms persist, adopting sustainable, organic practices that are attracting a growing number of consumers.

In the 1880s, Lyman C. Byce developed the Petaluma Incubator. Poultry and egg production grew to the point that Petaluma became known as "The World's Egg Basket." In 1945, sales of eggs reached a high of more than 52 million dozen. Then the cost of land and operations increased. Farm children sought more education and less tedious vocations. By the 1980s, the number of egg producers in the Petaluma area had dwindled from thousands to a few hundred. Yet, Petaluma's poultry and egg industry remains successful, building on the growing popularity of free range and certified organic chickens and eggs.

Fruit and vegetable farming is another area in which organic, sustainable practices are creating a future while preserving family farms. Large quantities of produce are no longer shipped away as they once were, but the quality of Petaluma area produce has brought some of the world's top chefs and finest restaurants here and attracted new residents and travelers from near and far.

Perhaps the newest star in the agricultural firmament is the wine industry. Almost wiped out by prohibition, local wineries are now producing sought-after wines that owe their unique quality to the cool evenings and morning fog of the Petaluma Gap.

Byce's incubator spurred Petaluma's first manufacturing boom. A century later, the "information superhighway" sliced through town, carving out Telecom Valley. Telecom Valley bloomed briefly and then faded, never quite reaching the level of economic success it promised. Lately, though, smaller high tech companies are popping up all around Petaluma, generating some very exciting ideas.

Spared by the 1906 earthquake, most of Petaluma's signature Victorian architecture has also been spared by new development. One of this book's contributors, Skip Sommer, was responsible for restoring the Great Petaluma Mill for use as offices, shops and restaurants.

Petaluma's largest redevelopment project, however, has just been completed. It includes several riverfront blocks just south of the historic downtown. Basin Street Properties has done an admirable job of preserving some existing buildings and blending them with architecture that captures much of the style of the warehouses they replaced.

Growth and change are always difficult. Here, as in many smaller cities, they are a constant source of controversy. We can take great pride in the fact that Petaluma was the first city in America to have a Supreme Court-approved plan to control residential growth. Within it, we've so far managed to embrace a burgeoning bedroom community, three historic districts, and many buildings that are listed on the National Register of Historic Places. Our economy successfully balances sustainable agriculture with growing high tech, service, restaurant, arts, and tourism sectors. As Petalumans, we take great pride in our community. We are unusual because we are an engaged citizenry, energetically supporting a wide range of causes — from youth programs to parks to the arts, neighborhood betterment, ecology and more.

As we look to the future, we have a lot to celebrate.

ONE

THE RIVER
by Bill Rhodes with additional information provided by the Petaluma Yacht Club

The Petaluma River became
the avenue of commerce
for food and lumber
moving to San Francisco
and beyond.

McNEAR FEED

150 YEARS

LOADING HAY

Long before the Miwok Indians arrived in this precious valley, the design for the future had already been well established. The land was fertile. The waterways and wetlands were teeming with fish and waterfowl. Elk and deer were plentiful and the climate was pristine.

The environment of the Petaluma Valley was the gift presented to our earliest inhabitants — as it is to those who come here today.

Some records show this area was inhabited as long as 5,000 years ago by ancestors of the Indian tribes that initially made this their home and gave names to the towns surrounding this beautiful valley. According to some sources Petaluma means "flat back," a reference to Sonoma Mountain. Cotati is Miwok for "a punch in the face," and Tomales comes from the Miwok for "west." Of course, these name origins are still in debate and probably always will be.

The Indians were kind to the land. They saw it as part of their existence. The salmon, the deer and the elk were part of a cycle of life in which they were participants. The Indians used no more than they needed and tried to leave no scars or evidence they had been there on the land.

Of course, the land was kind to the Indians in return. It has been reported that the Petaluma Valley supported as many as 16 Indians per square mile, versus an average of just one per square mile in Indian settlements elsewhere in the United States.

In the late 1700s and early 1800s, the Spanish claimed California and gave land grants to a favored few. This area was granted to General Mariano Vallejo. He said it well when he first set eyes on this valley in May, 1833: "I have made a visit to Paradise — the fairest land in all the world. Nothing in all California is comparable; everything is readymade for civilization — soil, climate, abundant water, a great harbor, opportunity for commerce with the world, and for landscape, for variety, a land of pure enchantment."

When Vallejo spoke of "the opportunity for commerce with the world," he was referring to the Petaluma River. Actually, it isn't really a river. It's a tidal slough — an arm of water that is fed by San Pablo Bay, rising and falling with the tide. But, proper river or not, one of Vallejo's first priorities was to build docks on an arm of the Petaluma River and to commence shipping cowhides to the Bay.

Before long, men from the gold fields began to arrive, drawn by the plentiful game. Settlers from the east arrived by wagon train as well, and stayed because the land was good for growing crops and grazing cattle.

The vast resources surrounding Petaluma helped to build the town into the center of commerce it became. The redwoods to the north built San Francisco, twice, once in the 1800s and again after the earthquake of 1906. The fields were perfect for growing hay, apples and grapes. The land closer to the coast was not so friendly for farming, but its proximity to the ocean, and the cooler, moister climate made perfect conditions for dairy farming. The grass stayed green longer into the summer and the cooler days made for contented cows. The Petaluma River became the avenue of commerce for food and lumber moving to San Francisco and beyond.

And for heaven's sake don't forget the eggs. Eggs and chickens had as much to do with the incredible growth of Petaluma as a hub of commerce as anything. However, if it weren't for the Petaluma River, all those eggs would have never made it to the market place. Boats used to transport eggs were of a special design, with the smokestack in the stern so heat from the engines would not poach the eggs in transport. Once again, the river proved itself to be the lifeblood of the town. At one time, as much freight moved up and down the Petaluma River as the Sacramento River. It's said that Petaluma was even considered once for the State Capital.

The port of Petaluma became increasingly crowded with incoming, loading, unloading and departing boats. Scows, schooners and steamers were, at times, moored two deep for two miles along the docks south of town. Three separate steamboats were christened "Petaluma" and two named "Gold." All eventually sank, exploded or burned. The remnants of one are sometimes still visible at low tide, as are the remnants of the first sternwheeler on the river, the first steamer "Gold."

Room to turn around and maneuver was in short supply and caused significant delays in shipping. So the decision was made by the pioneer entrepreneurs to make more room. It may be legend, but I have

SCOW-SCHOONERS LIKE THE "ALMA" WERE THE DELIVERY TRUCKS OF TURN-OF-THE-CENTURY SHIPPING BETWEEN PETALUMA AND SAN FRANCISCO. FLAT-BOTTOMED, THEY COULD NAVIGATE SHALLOW WATER, THEN REST SECURELY ON THE MUD ALONG THE BANKS WHILE LOADING AND UNLOADING CARGO.

TOM CORBETT

CLOCKWISE FROM LEFT: STEAMER "GOLD";
THE ORIGINAL DRAWBRIDGE ON WASHINGTON STREET;
THE 80-FOOT, SINGLE-LEAF BASCULE BRIDGE INSTALLED IN 1937 WAS
DESIGNED BY JOSEPH STRAUSS, WHO DESIGNED THE GOLDEN GATE BRIDGE;
WIDENED RIVER AFTER DREDGING.

heard Chinese laborers were brought in to dig away the earth from the point across from where the Petaluma Yacht Club is now located. They created the much larger open area now known as the Turning Basin. Boats and schooners could now pass each other getting to the docks and then turn around for the trip back down the river.

In the early years navigating the ever-changing twists and turns of the river was challenging, especially in fog or at night. One captain claimed to have 80 turns timed exactly so that he could make the trip even when there was no visibility. Later, many of the turns were eliminated. Four long, straight cuts were planned. Three were completed. Cut D, the closest to town, was dredged by the Army Corps of Engineers in about 1920. I have no dates for the dredging of cuts A and C further south. Cut B was never executed. Of course, wherever dredging is done, the river always tries to regain its "natural meander."

One "natural meander" was eliminated in digging off the point of land to create the Turning Basin. Every winter when it rains, silt comes down from the hills and the river tries to put the "meander" back where it was. Every four years or so, depending on the winters and the runoff, it is necessary to dredge the Turning Basin to maintain navigability.

If the dredging weren't done regularly, the river would try to return to its natural state and an island would begin to form where the point of land was. That, of course, would discourage pleasure boats from coming to town — and decrease the revenue they bring. In 1959, to facilitate the heavy commercial traffic, the Petaluma Creek was upgraded to "River" status by an act of Congress signed by President Eisenhower. With this designation, the Corps of Engineers was authorized to perform the dredging.

Today, the Turning Basin still serves its original purpose: to provide revenue-bearing craft with access to our town. They leave a great deal of their revenue here, as they always did. Only the things they buy and take away downriver have changed.

That is how it is, and that is how it should be. The Petaluma River was the conduit for the lifeblood of this community from the earliest times — centuries ago — and it continues to be one of our most important resources.

The advent of railroads and, then, rubber tires took the demand off the river as a trade route. Jerico Products still dredges ancient oyster shell in South San Francisco Bay for calcium for animal feeds. Shamrock Construction brings stone from around the world to Petaluma for processing into building materials. If the tonnage isn't maintained, the Corps of Engineers might not be able to justify regular dredging. For most of the last century, however, the amount of traffic on the river decreased substantially. This period of relative inactivity was actually a blessing for the river and for its tributaries and the marshlands to the south.

During this time, the city of Petaluma turned its back on the river. Merchants didn't need it as much for shipping anymore, so they began to ignore the river and to turn what was once a thriving riverfront into a backyard. The warehouses and docks and mills that lined the once bustling riverfront loading areas were gradually vacated, abandoned or converted to some other use. Many of the old buildings were torn down. However, until fairly recently, even new developments along the riverbanks turned their backs to the river. In some cases, developers actually planted trees and shrubs to screen their projects from the river. They didn't see the value of this incredible resource. The Golden

Today, the Turning Basin still serves its original purpose: to provide revenue-bearing craft with access to our town. They leave a great deal of their revenue here, as they always did. Only the things they buy and take away downriver have changed.

That is how it is, and that is how it should be. The Petaluma River was the conduit for the lifeblood of this community from the earliest times — centuries ago — and it continues to be one of our most important resources.

JERICO PRODUCTS TUGBOATS

Eagle Shopping Center existed for years before Dempsey's and the Waterfront Grill began to take advantage of their riverfront sites.

In some cases, river frontage became a dumpsite for worn out and unwanted items — boats, cars, tires, and anything else no longer needed. Fortunately for the river, this kind of abuse was limited.

In the 1970s, however, the city fathers began to reevaluate the potential of the riverfront and to consider renovation of some of the more substantial and significant buildings on the river. As fate would have it, a Marin County banker introduced them to a very successful Marin County developer. The developer was

Skip Sommer. The building he had in mind for renovation and repurposing was the Great Petaluma Mill. Ed Love was also instrumental in the renovation of the Great Petaluma Mill and numerous other projects associated with the riverfront renaissance.

Another visionary developer to come on the scene early in this renaissance was Walter Haake. Walter, too, came up from Marin County when he saw the potential of the historic warehouses along the river. The warehouses were situated so that freight could easily come and go by scow and schooner. Walter saw the location and orientation of the warehouses as a key element in his plan. Walter used access to the river and views of the river as tools to enhance his project. People are attracted to water, and that is certainly a major reason for the success of his "Foundry Wharf Business Park".

By the 1980s the Petaluma Yacht Club and the Petaluma Area Chamber of Commerce had joined together to entice boaters from all around the bay and delta to take weekend trips up the peaceful, beautiful, wildlife-rich Petaluma River.

They could dock at the turning basin where, just a few decades ago, commercial schooners and paddle wheelers jammed in to load or unload their cargo. From dockside, it would be a short walk to the unique shops, quality restaurants, and historic architecture of downtown Petaluma.

They came. They brought money. The transition from freight dollars to tourist dollars was underway.

THE GOLDEN EAGLE MILL PROPERTY BECAME THE SITE FOR THE GOLDEN EAGLE SHOPPING CENTER

In the early 1980s, the River Committee of the Petaluma Area Chamber of Commerce became a major catalyst in reestablishing the importance of the river. Our belief was that if we enhanced the river, businesses and the community would benefit. A group of business owners, property owners, organizations, and individuals was assembled to chart a course of progress for the river's future.

Then came the Petaluma River Festival. Among those who joined me in the efforts to establish this festival were Ed Love, Lyndi Brown, Maria Warren Tabarria, Susan Warren Villa, Fred Schram, Al Alys, Alice Forsyth, Marie Mitchell, Rowene Brewer, Peter Markey, and Skip Sommer. The event was designed to bring the residents of Petaluma down to the river. More specifically, our aim was to get as many as possible ON the river.

I had discovered for myself that it's impossible to *APPRECIATE* the Petaluma River if you haven't been *ON* the Petaluma River. It's necessary to go downstream a ways — past the old buildings, docks and industrial sites. It's necessary to glide silently through the relatively pristine marshlands that border the river as it meanders

It's necessary to glide silently through the relatively pristine marshlands
that border the river as it meanders slowly and quietly towards San Pablo Bay.
You will see and hear all forms of wildlife along your journey.
There will be ducks, geese, egrets, pipers, hawks and on and on.

CROWDS AT THE RIVERFEST IN 1986

slowly and quietly towards San Pablo Bay. You will see and hear all forms of wildlife along your journey. There will be ducks, geese, egrets, pipers, hawks and on and on. You may possibly even get a glimpse of a fox. From San Pablo Bay, you could continue across to San Francisco or, for that matter, head out the Golden Gate and around the world.

We thought we'd be lucky to draw a thousand people to the first Petaluma River Festival in 1986. More than 10,000 turned out, and the festival continued successfully for more than a decade.

It can be seen from the attention given the river in the drafting of Petaluma's award-winning General Plan of 1986, that it had gained a position of significant importance to the future of the city.

One of the specific "Central Goals" of the plan was to "Enhance the river as a resource to be preserved, seen, and used." In the chapter that addressed the river, the plan stated, "The Petaluma River should be a place of activity and a source of open space and vistas for all Petalumans." Maximum public access, open views, water-oriented activities, a riverfront park with cultural facilities, and pedestrian

and bicycle routes along the river were all specific goals — as well as improving water quality and maintaining wildlife habitats and the natural setting.

As a result of the aggressive position taken by the River Committee of the Chamber of Commerce, the focus on the Petaluma River as an asset by the Petaluma River Festival, and the goals of the 1986 General Plan, there has been a great deal of activity on and around the river in the past two decades.

To protect both commercial and recreational interests in the river, a River Chapter Subcommittee of the General Plan Update Committee was formed. It had become obvious that the river was a valuable resource to this community and the Bay Area. In fact, the Petaluma River was the focus of one entire chapter in the General Plan Update. Here are some excerpts from that chapter:

> "The significance of the Petaluma River lies in its roles as a natural habitat, a carrier of flood waters, a centerpiece of urban identity and local history, a recreation resource, and a waterway of potential beauty."

> "The River is a prominent visual resource that can continue to add to the city's identity."

The goals spelled out in this chapter give the city direction on how to realize that vast potential we have in our waterway.

> Goal 1: Develop recreational and cultural opportunities along the Petaluma River in a manner sensitive to the environment.

> Goal 2: Preserve and protect the Petaluma River and streams in their natural state as open spaces, natural resources and habitats.

> Goal 3: Maintain the Petaluma River as a navigable river to the head of navigation.

The next section, "Reclaiming the Waterfront," provides specific recommendations for waterfront usage. It states that recreational and cultural activities are needed and that the turning basin could be a lively complement to downtown activity. It further states that opportunities to see and have access to the river should be increased.

ABOVE: AT THE SITE OF A SMALL BOAT LAUNCHING RAMP, THE PETALUMA MARINA OPENED IN 1990

BELOW: THE TURNING BASIN AT SUNSET

That section of the plan

also suggested a pedestrian bridge to circulate foot traffic from the Golden Eagle Shopping Center to the Historic Downtown. The Balshaw Bridge, named after a staunch river proponent and City Councilman, was built in 1989. It's hard, now, to imagine what we did without it. These are some of the recommendations included in the section on "Objectives, Policies and Programs":

DEDICATION OF THE BALSHAW BRIDGE, 1989

BILL RHODES

JIM JOHNSON, STUDIO 7

(a) Insure public access to the Petaluma River along the full length of the river where feasible.

(b) Create a riverfront route for pedestrians and bicyclists on both sides of the river.

(c) Open up views of the river.

(d) Preserve and protect the Petaluma River as open space, resource and habitat.

(e) Preserve and protect streams and the river in their natural state.

Policy 1: As development and redevelopment occur, the City shall require public access to the Petaluma River from the nearest public street and walkways. "Development" includes the subdivision of land.

Policy 2: The City shall enhance the Petaluma River and its banks as a scenic resource consistent with water-oriented recreation.

Policy 7: Appropriate efforts shall be made to expose the river to public view.

Policy 8: New development or redevelopment with river frontage shall face both the river and the street on which it is located.

There are many more examples of this kind of thinking and planning outlined in the rest of the chapter on the river and open spaces.

PETALUMA RIVER CLEAN-UP DAY (BOTH PHOTOS)

COURTESY PETALUMA RIVER CLEANUP COMMITTEE

COURTESY PETALUMA RIVER CLEANUP COMMITTEE

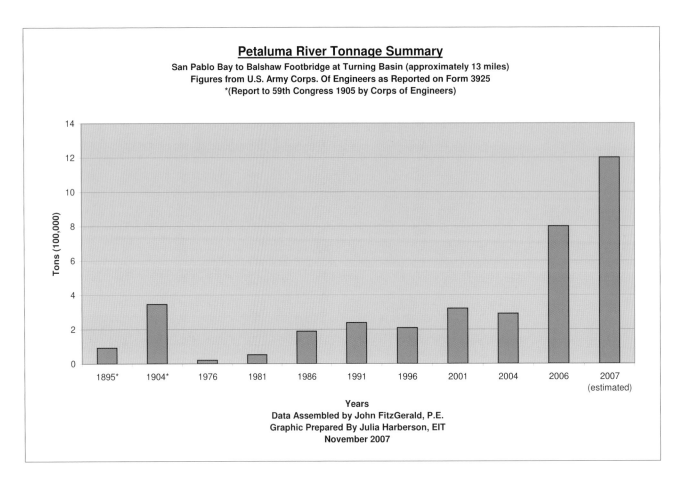

Petaluma River Tonnage Summary
San Pablo Bay to Balshaw Footbridge at Turning Basin (approximately 13 miles)
Figures from U.S. Army Corps. Of Engineers as Reported on Form 3925
*(Report to 59th Congress 1905 by Corps of Engineers)

Years
Data Assembled by John FitzGerald, P.E.
Graphic Prepared By Julia Harberson, EIT
November 2007

The future of the Petaluma River has been well charted by a number of interested and concerned civic leaders, businesses, citizens and groups. All seem to share common goals: conservation, preservation, education, protection, enhancement, safe and enjoyable recreation, and continued commercial use.

These groups include Friends of the Petaluma River, Petaluma River Festival, Petaluma Area Chamber of Commerce River Committee, Petaluma River Works, The Bay Institute, San Francisco Bay Joint Venture, Bay Area Audubon Council, the Petaluma River Cleanup Committee, the Petaluma River Authority, Petaluma Small Craft Center, and the No Wetlands Landfill Expansion group. In addition to these recreation-focused groups, there continue to be businesses that use the river for commercial purposes — such as Jerico Products, Dutra Materials and Shamrock Materials. The tonnage of goods shipped up and down the Petaluma River has always been of paramount importance because it's the reason that the river is routinely dredged. By all estimates this tonnage will continue its historical growth.

It is clear that Petalumans have an appreciation for their river as a historical and current asset, and that diligent work to sustain it is required. A healthy river is part of a healthy community.

If you build camp on the banks of a river and the river rises, you're going to get your feet wet. If the river you're camping alongside rises twice a day because of the design of the waterway — or the seasonal rains are heavy — then it makes sense that your chances of getting wet are even better.

THE PETALUMA RIVER AND SAN PABLO BAY FROM LAFFERTY RANCH

SCOTT HESS

Don't build in the flood plain. You cannot control the waterways when they decide to breach, no matter what you have constructed to hold them back. Period.

So flood control seems to be in order. How do you control flooding? You don't. You can't control Mother Nature. All that can be sensibly done is to realize that flooding will sometimes occur and camp where your chances of getting wet are minimized.

Ranchers, farmers, individuals, little cities, big cities, and on and on have tried for decades to "control flooding," but they have all failed in time — because occasional flooding is the nature of Mother Nature. No matter how good the plans and constructions of man, she always prevails.

A "blue ribbon committee" was appointed by President Clinton after major flooding in the Midwest had occurred during his administration. The committee was non-partisan and focused on how to resolve the problem of flooding in our cities. Their findings were obvious: Don't build in the flood plain. You cannot control the waterways when they decide to breach, no matter what you have constructed to hold them back. Period.

Education is expensive. One way or the other you pay for it. Petaluma has paid for camping next to the river more than once. Residents and businesses alike have paid dearly. We've had to move houses away from the riverbanks. We've lost revenue and suffered damage to goods and property.

So the answer is clear. Stay back from the river. Make the most of what it is — a wonderful gift from Mother Nature. Sit back and create ways to enjoy it from a little distance. Use the areas along the river for recreation, parks, natural habitat, walkways and bikeways. Let them be a place for the river to overflow in the winter, because it will.

JO ANN NAYLOR

TWO

THE LAST WOMAN FROM PETALUMA
by Greg Sarris

Her Indian name,
or at least one of her Indian names,
the only one any of us know,
was Tsupu.

She was my great-great-grandfather's mother, or my great-great-great grandmother, and (again as far as any of us know) the last native of Petaluma — not the city we know today, but the ancient Coast Miwok village of the same name. Certainly, she was the last to pass down any memory of the place. She was quite young, perhaps fourteen, when she left, beginning what would become a chaotic and wholly incredible journey to find and keep a home in and about Sonoma County. Though the village was abandoned once and for all after the 1838 smallpox epidemic claimed its remaining citizens and though American farmers demolished its large midden — using the centuries-old refuge of decomposed shells for fertilizer and eradicating any trace of the village — Tsupu never forgot it. The last time she visited, she was completely blind, yet nodding with her chin to an empty hillside, she said "there," as if she could see Petaluma plain as day, tule huts and fire smoke.

The village was atop a low hill, east of the Petaluma River, located about three and a half miles northeast of the present city of Petaluma. "Petaluma" in Coast Miwok means "sloping ridge," and, as was often the custom, it was no doubt named after that distinct feature of the landscape associated with its location. C. Hart Merriam, a naturalist interested in the Indians of California, wrote in 1907 that "the name Petaluma appears to have come from the Kanamara Pomo (South Pomo) on the north," but, as linguist Catherine A. Callaghan points out, "Petaluma" is clearly a Coast Miwok word: *peta•luma*: slope ridge.

There was never a tribe or nation known as Coast Miwok; the aboriginal people of Petaluma never referred to themselves as such. Linguists and anthropologists, classifying California natives at the turn of the 20th century by language families, identified the dozen or more distinct aboriginal nations ranging from the southern Santa Rosa plain to the northern tip of the San Francisco Bay as "Coast Miwok" speakers, as opposed to "Pomo" speakers to the north and "Wappo" speakers to the east. While variations in the languages of the Pomo-speaking nations were in some cases so great that different nations could not understand one another, such was not the case with Coast Miwok speakers. Variations were mostly in accent, as between British English and American English — and were never more diverse than Old English and Modern English — allowing Coast Miwok nations to communicate freely with one another.

Petaluma, a thriving community of at least 500 individuals, was a major village of the *Lekatuit* Nation, whose territory included the Petaluma Valley and extended north and west to *Potaawa · yowa*, or

"Petaluma" in Coast Miwok means "sloping ridge,"
and, as was often the custom, it was no doubt named after that distinct
feature of the landscape associated with its location.

Chalk Ground, another large Lekatuit village, once located near the present town of Freestone. Lekatuit — which means "cross-ways willow" in Coast Miwok — was also the name of a village located just a half mile north of the present town of Petaluma, actually closer than the aboriginal village of the same name.

The Petaluma Valley region was prized for its enormous herds of deer and elk as well as for its productive groves of valley oak and black oak. Coast Miwok elder Maria Copa (from Nicasio) told anthropologist Isabel Kelly in 1932 that "deer and elk used to be plentiful in the valley this side of Petaluma [present city] — just like cattle there [and that] Nicasio people got acorns from the Petaluma Valley." Ducks and geese flew up from the Petaluma River and its tributaries so thick as to obliterate the sun for an hour at a time, and seasonal swarms of monarch butterflies passing through the Petaluma Valley a mile wide and several miles long forced the Lekatuit there to take refuge for sometimes a full day. Petaluma, the ancient village, was situated along a major trade route that stretched south and west through other Coast Miwok villages, north into Pomo territory and east into Wappo and Wintun territories. The region's abundant deer and elk and acorn supply positioned its people well to trade for what they needed from other places. And Petaluma was considered a sacred place. On a low hill opposite the hill on which the village was located, Coyote — that sometimes foolish Creator-figure for most California Indian

TOM SMITH IN ABOUT 1900

tribes — had his conversation with Chicken Hawk about creating human beings. Again, Maria Copa said, "It was at *wotoke*, a place near Petaluma, that Coyote and *walinapi* [Chicken Hawk] talked first. Coyote was living on a rock on top of that hill."

Tom Smith, my great-great-grandfather, told Isabel Kelly that his mother "was half Petaluma, half Tomales, half Bodega." Despite Tom Smith's problematic math and the fact that no information can be found in mission or church records regarding Tsupu's parents (or, for that matter, Tsupu) one can surmise that it was Tsupu's father who was from Petaluma, since the custom held that after marriage women joined the husband's family. Tsupu later settled in *Eye · kotca*, or Fruit House, a post-European contact makeshift village in Coleman Valley, in the heart of Bodega Miwok, or Olamentke, territory, where her mother, Tom Smith's grandmother, and his uncles had houses and where Tom Smith was born and grew up. Tsupu's mother more than likely came from Olamentke Nation then, though from which village remains unknown.

Tsupu is the Coast Miwok word for "wild cucumber." A poultice can be made from the plant's juices as an antidote for boils; the word was sometimes used for "boils" and then again for "a cure for boils." Coast Miwok people had many nicknames. Whether Tsupu was a nickname or a proper name isn't clear. At some point she was baptized Maria, and even later was referred to as Maria Chekka, or Cheka, suggesting Russian influence, and Maria Chica, suggesting Spanish or Mexican influence. She was also known both as Miss Comtechal and Miss Smith. Ultimately, she had six children and scores of grandchildren and great-grandchildren, and perhaps the many families had as many different names for her. In my family, she was called "Little Grandma." Perhaps she was quite small, shrunken in age, and remembered that way, or maybe she had always been a petite woman.

Marguerite Huguez, who told me what little was left in the family about Tsupu, was my father's first cousin and lived her entire life in East Los Angeles, specifically Boyle Heights, where both she and my father were born after their mothers escaped Sherman Indian School in the 1920s. "Grandma used to talk a little bit about 'Little Grandma,'" Marguerite said, closing her eyes as if to drown out the noisy street beyond her front door and picture a woman she had never seen — her grandmother's grandmother. It was a hot, uncomfortable afternoon in 1987, twenty years ago, and I wanted to go as far back and learn as much about my family history as possible. Marguerite, self-described as having been a nosey child, was the eldest in my family of my father's generation and seemed to have a better sense of family history than anyone else. "Grandma was young when she [Little Grandma] died," Marguerite added. Then all at once she opened her eyes, looking about the room surprised, as if she had awakened suddenly and found herself lost. She looked north, away from me, and said, "It was somewhere up there."

Marguerite said that when Tsupu died she was wearing her finest clothes, a handmade late 19th century black dress with a bustle and fitted bodice and a silk mantilla from the Mexican California period that covered her face and reached to the ground, as if she had dressed for her own funeral. Regardless of whether or not Tsupu was always a small woman, she must have been attractive, even beautiful. She would win the heart of Bodega Bay's most important citizen.

When Tsupu

was born, by any estimate about 1820, the village of Petaluma was in crisis. At least a third of its citizens had died within the last ten years of European diseases — smallpox, pneumonia, syphilis — to which the natives had no resistance. The great herds of deer and elk, frightened by blasts from Spanish muskets, were scattering, migrating north, replaced by mission livestock — cattle, horses, sheep — which spread foreign seed in dung, giving rise to oat grass, among other invasive species, which supplanted the native bunch grasses and sedges. The Lekatuit, like other California aboriginal nations, had had an intimate relationship with their environment, specifically a seasonal schedule of harvesting, pruning, controlled burning and the like, from which a particular and sustainable ecology had evolved over 5,000 years or more. With fewer individuals to tend the landscape, or garden, as we liked to call it, and with a major disruption of native animal and plant habitats, the valley began to appear "wild."

Coast Miwok show up on mission records as early as 1786, and in great numbers from 1795 to 1803, but these individuals were largely from southern nations — Huimen, Gualen, and Aguasto. The Spanish made their first incursions into the Petaluma Valley, looking in earnest for Indian recruits for Mission Dolores, in 1814, the year "Petalumas" first appear on mission records. Yet relatively few "Petalumas" were baptized in the mission, and few "Petalumas" resided in Mission San Rafael, which was established in 1817 after Spanish soldiers had pushed much further north into southern Pomo territory. The Lekatuit, like their southern Pomo neighbors, were known among the Spanish as "rebellious." No doubt, word of mouth from the southern Coast Miwok nations regarding the mistreatment of Indians in the missions impeded the soldiers' attempts to coerce the Lekatuit and southern Pomo from their villages.

The Lekatuit villagers of Petaluma struggled to maintain traditional lifeways. Tsupu would be schooled by grandparents, as was the custom, specifically by her grandmother (her father's mother), who was born and came of age in Petaluma before European contact — or at least before European contact created significant change and stress in the village. She learned basket weaving, when and where to gather sedge, bulrush, and willow for baskets. She learned when and where to gather acorns, various seeds for pinole, pinenuts, roots, clovers, over two hundred herbs. She learned how to construct a tule *kotca*, or house, and how to make women's skirts from tule and sew rabbit skins for blankets. She listened to stories. She learned to read the landscape and know its songs. She learned the powers associated with mountains, rocks, streams, an owl or raven's call, clouds and fog, angles of the sun and moon, and the shifting map of stars in the nighttime sky.

Petaluma, like most other Coast Miwok villages, was governed by a nonhereditary headman — known as the *hoipu* — and at least two female leaders, or headwomen. The most powerful was known as the *maien*, who, as Tom Smith told Isabel Kelly, "bosses everyone, even hoipu." Anyone — but usually a father — could nominate a young man for the position of hoipu, but a committee of four older women not only chose the candidate but was responsible for training him in the art of leadership as well, further illustrating the primacy of women in Coast Miwok government. Because physical warfare was considered the lowest form of power, demonstrating only that an individual possessed no secret spiritual powers to draw upon and therefore could be assaulted without fear of spiritual retribution referred to as "poisoning," and because women were considered to have an abundance of spiritual powers, usually more than men, rape was unheard of. While men usually hunted important ceremonial birds — woodpeckers, mallard ducks, ravens, condors — it was the women who made the elaborately designed ceremonial capes, skirts, and headdresses from the feathers.

Petaluma had two primary subdivisions, or moieties, within the village, known as "Land" and "Water," which correlated with, and hence connected the villagers to, the same two moieties in other Lekatuit villages and Coast Miwok nations. The moieties helped maintain cohesion between nations and were important when selecting a marriage partner. After her first menses, when she would have been put in a bed of warm sand for five days, Tsupu was tattooed with slight, zigzagging lines extending from each corner of her mouth to below her chin, indicating not only her village and nation but also her moiety. Tsupu, whether a proper name given 30 days after her birth or a nickname, is a Land name. After her first menses, she would have been given another Land name, albeit a secret name, perhaps selected and thus known only by members of a special women's society.

Empowered individuals, Petaluma women were clever and resourceful, and Tsupu must have watched as her grandmother artfully negotiated traditional culture and values amidst Spanish disruption. But neither would escape unscathed the next, and more violent, wave of immigrants.

Missions San Rafael and Solano (in Sonoma) were secularized by the Mexican government in 1834. Mexican General Mariano Vallejo had already established a military base at Mission Solano a year earlier. Impressed by General Vallejo's military prowess and anxious to limit Russian expansion from Fort Ross on the north coast, Governor José Figueroa of Monterey rewarded Vallejo with title to a ten-league grant known as Rancho Petaluma, about 60,000 acres stretching from Lekatuit territory in the west to Mission Solano in the east. General Vallejo built his Rancho headquarters, an adobe fort, on the grasslands in eastern Lekatuit territory.

The Mexicans established an elaborate slave trade, buying and selling Native men and boys on ranchos, often as far away as Mexico. Mexican soldiers weren't different from their Spanish predecessors, who, as historian Alan Rosenus notes in *General Vallejo And The Advent Of The Americas*, "assumed that the exploitation of Indian women was a right of conquest." Sometime in the first days of the Rancho, a soldier found a young girl about fourteen years old. She was not a neophyte from the missions in dirty clothing looking for food and work, but a native — bare breasted in a tule skirt, barefoot — and they hauled her into the fort. She was Tsupu. What happened there no one knows. Nor does anyone know how long — days, weeks — she stayed. She escaped, kept an eye open for the unlatched door or sleeping guard, and began a fifty-mile trek north to Fort Ross — perhaps seeing her village as she

Marguerite said that when Tsupu died she was wearing her finest clothes, a handmade late 19th century black dress with a bustle and fitted bodice and a silk mantilla from the Mexican California period that covered her face and reached to the ground, as if she had dressed for her own funeral.

passed in the dark of night. Her last memory of Petaluma, then, was of a place of shadows.

Tsupu's journey, whether alone or with other escapees, had to have been difficult. More than likely she traveled west from the Rancho fort to the coast, following a route she had used many times with other Petaluma villagers to trade with Olamentke villagers for Washington clam shells (used as currency when ground into dime-sized discs) and to fish and gather seaweed. Again, Tsupu's mother had come from an Olamentke village, and Tsupu therefore must have had relatives within the coastal villages. But the land was rife with Mexican soldiers, besides those who may have pursued Tsupu, as well as with early Americans, who could surely take advantage of a fourteen-year-old Indian girl defenseless in the brush. Juana Bautista, Maria Copa's mother and the last maien of the Nicasio village, told of being so frightened once at the sound of approaching horses that she lay face down in a dry creek bed and didn't look up, even as she was loaded onto a wagon bed, until she was back at Nicasio several hours later and realized it was her relatives who had picked her up.

After Tsupu forded the Russian River and found herself in Kashaya Pomo territory, following the coastline north toward Fort Ross, the landscape would become increasingly unfamiliar to her. If roving Mexican soldiers and a foreign landscape made the journey dangerous, so too did the animals, particularly grizzly bears, which — like other powerful creatures on the land — no longer enjoyed age old agreements with humans regarding shared habitats. Thus disrupted and hostile, they posed a serious threat to unarmed passersby.

In 1834, Fort Ross was a well-established settlement, the Russians' southernmost outpost of a colonial empire that reached from the Siberian peninsula. The colony's census indicates nearly a hundred Native women (mostly Kashaya Pomo and Coast Miwok from Bodega and Jenner) and relatively few Native men residing at the Fort. Some of the Native men may have been on boats, scanning the coastline for sea otters with the Aleut hunters who had accompanied the Russian hunters and soldiers to Fort Ross from Alaska. But, more than likely, the greater number of Native women at Fort Ross had to do with its economy. Native women tended the colony's wheat fields and orchards and served as domestics, cooking and washing clothes for its nearly all male foreign population. Kashaya Pomo and Coast Miwok women were often concubines, if not regular wives, even as they maintained relationships, sometimes tenuously, with their Native husbands, whose usefulness around the Fort was largely limited to seasonal hunting and fishing, and who, as a result, remained at their respective indigenous villages, quite often raising the mixed-blood children born at the colony.

Indians trapped on Mexican ranchos considered Fort Ross a sanctuary. The Russians, for political reasons, armed the Natives against the Mexicans. While the Russians expected the Natives to work long hours, they usually did not mistreat them as the Mexicans had, and the Russians, members of the Orthodox Church, weren't interested in converting the Natives, leaving them to their indigenous religious practices.

Because many Native women at Fort Ross were Olamentke, Tsupu no doubt found relatives when she arrived, certainly women who spoke her language. Apparently, she learned the ropes at the colony rather quickly. She not only assumed duties such as gardening, washing clothes, tanning hides, and making tallow for soap and candles, but also found a non-resident Native husband with whom she established, as it would turn out, a lasting relationship. His name was Comtechal, a Russian name, perhaps a Russian pronunciation of an Indian word or name. He was of mixed parentage. His mother was Olamentke — originally from *Tókau*, a village on the east side of the Bodega peninsula—and his father was "Creole" — a Russian term for mixed-blood Natives, in this case a man whose mother was Kashaya Pomo and father half Russian, half Aleut. Even before the Russians abandoned the colony in 1842, Tsupu had left the Fort and settled with Comtechal at *Eye·kotca*, or Fruit House, the makeshift village north of Bodega Bay in Coleman Valley. They lived with Comtechal's mother and two brothers, and that is where the last of their three children, Tomas Comtechal (my great-great grandfather), was born in 1838 — hardly four years after Tsupu had left Petaluma.

When the Russians abandoned Fort Ross, after depleting the sea otter population upon which the colony was dependent for pelt trade with China, the Natives were left prey to marauding bands of Mexicans and early American settlers looking for Indian slaves. This was a most horrific period; Indians unable to seek protection on Mexican ranches, or as property of American squatters who "owned" the Indians in exchange for their labor, risked being captured and sold.

Comtechal's mother's family had settled at *Eye ·kotca* probably because of its remote location tucked in the rugged coastal hills and surrounded by gigantic redwoods. But even *Eye ·kotca* must have been threatened as more and more foreigners poured into the region.

Early in 1844, Stephen Smith, an American sea captain from Boston, arrived in Bodega Bay with a 35,787 acre land grant from the Mexican government. He also had with him his fifteen-year-old Peruvian wife — necessary as Mexican law stipulated an American must have "a Spanish spouse" in order to obtain a land grant. Already nearly sixty years old, Captain Smith wasted no time establishing a successful business, if not an empire. In 1846 he was appointed the "civil magistrate" for the region by the Mexican government; that same year, he built in the town of Bodega a sawmill operated by the first steam engine in California. A couple of years later, he survived the Bear Flag revolt, retaining ownership of his sawmill and a large portion of his vast acreage. At one point during the revolt, Americans reportedly took some of his horses (which they later returned) and many Indians who had sought refuge under him fled. But not the young Indian woman from Petaluma; she didn't leave. The Americans wouldn't touch her. They would no sooner bother her than bother Captain Smith's wife. Tsupu wasn't mere property, a concubine. She was the mother of Smith's only children and he loved her.

How Tsupu

and Captain Stephen Smith met no one knows. Captain Smith was rumored to be a good man, kind to the Indians. Moreover, he employed them on his rancho and in his mill, thus affording them both a living and protection from slave traders. Perhaps Tsupu, after a trek from *Eye ·kotca*, showed up outside his gate looking for work one morning — joining the line of Indians that showed up outside his gate looking for work every morning — and Captain Smith, needing a housekeeper, picked her out of the line, perhaps with a couple of other Indian women. Perhaps he took notice of her skill with an iron and broom, which she had honed at Fort Ross, and seeing her thus, he then saw her actual beauty, maybe heard the sound of her voice or discovered the way she moved, whatever might fancy a man, and then he couldn't help himself. Or maybe he saw her just once, passing on a road or trail, and that was it, his composure undermined then and there. Whatever the case, it wasn't long before she was a permanent resident on his rancho,

not in any makeshift Indian village or work camp, but less than two hundred feet from his house in his three-story barn, wherein he had fashioned for her an eight room home, with a kitchen, bedrooms, formal dining room and parlor — all on polished redwood slab floors. She continued to work, albeit as a supervisor of housekeepers and gardeners. That may have been what prompted the other Indians to begin referring to her as "maien." After she had children from him, three all together, he insisted she keep regular help in her home and a ninth room, a servant's quarters, was added in the barn.

The first piece of legislation that California enacted after it became a state in 1850 was the Act for Government and Protection of Indians, which stipulated that Indians became the rightful property of whose land they resided on, essentially legalizing Indian slavery (the law was repealed in 1868)." Captain Smith's Indians — most of whom were Olamentke and those like Tsupu who had fled north from other Coast Miwok nations — were safe, particularly under the watchful eye not of the Captain but of his mistress. Tsupu's first three children remained at *Eye ·kotca* with their father, Comtechal. Yet each of those children, no doubt for purposes of safety, adopted the name Smith. Hence my great-great grandfather, Tomás Comtechal, became Thomas, or Tom, Smith. Local Indians, when approached by American settlers, learned to say "Smith," guaranteeing their freedom.

By the time Stephen Smith died in 1855, Tsupu had secured such a position of influence throughout the region that Americans, seeing her approach in horse and buggy, tipped their hats in respect, often confusing her for his actual wife, who rarely left the house. Tsupu's power didn't wane, partly because she had established a good relationship with Captain Smith's widow (who obviously knew of her husband's liaison, seeing the mixed-blood children about the place). Perhaps, rather than being jealous, she had been relieved by his affections for the Indian woman. Before she left the rancho about 1870, moving to San Francisco where she would spend the rest of her life, Captain Smith's widow made provisions for Tsupu and her family to reside on her late husband's property and deeded a two acre plot overlooking Bodega Bay to the "Smith Family" for a cemetery.

Did Tsupu love Captain Smith? The nature of their relationship is no more known than is the manner in which they came together in the first place. While Tsupu became acquainted with and probably wore Western clothing at Fort Ross, she learned elements of fashion

GENE BUVOLET

when she became involved with Captain Smith. She was adept to the extent that, in hats and showy frocks, she appeared equal to her status as mistress of the most influential man in Bodega. She became proficient in Spanish and English, and she already spoke Russian. But she never forgot her Coast Miwok ways. She wove baskets with designs distinctive to her Petaluma village and Lekatuit nation. In the hills and gullies, she cut willow branches and, along the creeks, found sedge roots which she split with her teeth into long, fine strands, necessary for the watertight baskets that fewer and fewer Coast Miwok women could weave. She harvested acorns each fall from under the coastal tan oaks. Even late in her life, she was seen often with a stone pestle pounding acorns into fine meal in a stone mortar, or leaching the meal with water over a circular bed of coarse sand. And she never stopped returning to *Eye·kotca*, to see not only her children there, but also Comtechal. Eventually, the village of *Eye·kotca* was abandoned. Comtechal moved to *Tawak·puluk*, or Shoulder Bone Pond, the location of an ancient Olamentke summer village about three-quarters of a mile north of Bodega Bay. Not long after Captain Smith's widow moved to San Francisco, Tsupu joined Comtechal at *Tawak·puluk*, in a one-room cabin. She would remain there for almost thirty years, until he died, two weeks before she died.

Tom Smith became the last Coast Miwok medicine man, and he is reputed to have caused the 1906 earthquake in a contest of power with another medicine man, Big Jose, from the Kashaya Pomo Nation.

William Smith, the youngest child of Tsupu and Captain Stephen Smith, built a large house at Bodega Bay, where his sons established and operated a lucrative fishing business for many years. Today more than 500 individuals trace their ancestry to Tsupu, about the same number of Lekatuit living in the ancient village of Petaluma at the time of European contact. My cousin, Kathleen Smith, a talented artist and descendent of William Smith, demonstrates acorn preparation in Bay Area schools and parks, pounding and leaching acorns as her great-great-grandmother once had with her grandmother along the Petaluma River a hundred and seventy-five years ago.

Tsupu must've talked about the ancient village. She must've talked about the oak trees and the deer and elk there. Maybe she talked about her family, people she knew — and maybe she told Coyote stories her grandmother told her. What people remember her saying, what she talked about for the longest time, was the condors, or rather the absence of them. She probably didn't return to the Petaluma Valley until the 1870s, long enough after the Act for Government and Protection of Indians was repealed and she could travel safely where she wasn't known, beyond the confines of Captain Smith's rancho. By then the Petaluma region had changed radically. The immense redwood forests on the western hills were gone (Captain Smith clear-cut hills throughout Bodega and as far south as Petaluma). Most of the oak groves were gone. What few elk remained in Sonoma County now inhabited an area around the Laguna de Santa Rosa. Startled waterfowl didn't obscure the sun. There were farms and a town. Condors, those remarkable creatures with wing spans of up to 14 feet, whose feathers the Lekatuit used for ceremonial capes and aprons, were last seen in Coast Miwok territory in 1847, when citizens of Fairfax observed "more than a dozen." In 1860, in nearby Contra Costa County, "a bird with a wing span of thirteen and a half feet was spotted." Certainly, Tsupu would have noticed the absence of condors before. But even as her wagon reached the western edge of Petaluma Valley, she mentioned the condors, as if she hadn't until then noticed the empty sky. "How are the people going to dance without feathers?" she asked.

Did she mention the condors on her last trip to Petaluma, when my great-grandmother sat next to her on the wagon? Could she tell as much even though she was blind? Even blind, she knew the route well. Perhaps she had made several trips back to Petaluma by then. She died less than a year after that last trip. Marguerite told me that she was barefoot, sitting in a chair next to Comtechal's empty pallet, before she died. I see her like that, the last woman of Petaluma, barefoot, in a black dress, a floor-length mantilla already covering her face, sitting certain of the only thing besides her commitment to her children and Comtechal that she wouldn't have to second guess. But Marguerite would tell me she was certain of something else. On that last trip, after she nodded with her chin to the location of her village, the family turned the wagon around and then stopped in the town, before heading west back to Bodega. "We're in Petaluma," someone informed her. She became indignant. "No," she corrected, "we left it back there."

TOM SMITH

COURTESY DAVID PERI

THREE

THE EARLY YEARS
by Skip Sommer

In 1836, General Mariano Vallejo had built the first house in the Petaluma Valley and claimed rights to a vast piece of wilderness covered with oak and redwood and bordered by the Petaluma Creek.

GENERAL
MARIANO
VALLEJO

John Fritsch

JOHN FRITSCH

Petaluma Creek is a

tributary of San Pablo Bay. In 1848, it was navigable, at high tide, for small craft and scows of shallow draft for about 16 miles upstream. Debris, mud, and manure had not spoiled this pristine marshland at that time, and the water was fairly clear, attracting great schools of steelhead and sturgeon. The sky was often filled with clouds of feathered game of every description and deer, elk, antelope, bear and lion roamed freely. Wild grapes, blackberries, apples and oats made living pretty good for the peaceful Miwoks and Pomos. Unfortunately, thousands of these gentle people died in the white man's smallpox epidemic in 1838.

In 1836, General Mariano Vallejo had built the first house in the Petaluma Valley and claimed rights to a vast piece of wilderness covered with oak and redwood and bordered by the Petaluma Creek. Twelve years later, the California Gold Rush brought tens of thousands of men from around the world. When the "Rush" ended, many of the men stayed in the West, and many of them filtered into the Petaluma Valley.

Some "49ers" had been wildly successful and brought gold with which to buy boats and land. Most, though, were disappointed and looking for any way to make a living. Gradually, huts, shanties, beached boats, tents and primitive cabins started springing up on the banks of the creek.

Then Tom Lockwood, who had sailed around Cape Horn to get to the gold fields, traveled up Petaluma Creek in a sailing whaleboat to hunt for game. He and his friends were heavily armed with rifles and shotguns. At that time, a deer carcass went for $20 in San Francisco, a dozen quail brought $9, and if you could bag a wild cow, it was worth $80 in Sacramento. That was big money in those days.

Lockwood and friends set up a permanent camp on the bank of the creek. They were joined by a fellow named Pendleton, a sailor named Levi Pyburn, and two very talented men named Tom Bayliss and David Flogdell. Bayliss had been indentured to a sea captain on a voyage from Australia in 1847. The captain died along the way, freeing Bayliss from indenture. Bayliss and his shipmate, Flogdell, decided to stay in San Francisco. In 1849, they also sailed up the creek to hunt.

They all camped together and pooled their valuables, muscle and talents. Some had brought rope and gunpowder. Some had kettles and skillets. Some had barrels of provisions. Some had whiskey and tallow and mules. One had a violin. They all had guns, knives and axes and they all knew how to use them. It was an ambitious, tough group.

On the other side of the creek, Dr. August Heyermann built a log cabin. He had been successful in the gold fields and set out to buy a great estate, as well as to practice some medicine. Heyermann had been a "trail physician" for a large wagon train. It was a lot of work for little money. His easiest job was to dispense opium for 25 cents a dose to kill pain. Opium was very popular and dispensing it staked Heyermann to mining equipment.

These were the men who gave Petaluma its start as a shipping point. They helped each other in day-to-day living: splitting logs, caulking boats, repairing wagons, bringing in fresh water, digging wells and building outhouses — and, of course, they trapped and shot game and shipped it down the creek.

Meanwhile, Sacramento and San Francisco were growing fast. The cities traded such things as matches, cigars, crockery, tin ware and cloth for meat from up Petaluma Creek. By 1850, Bayliss and Flogdell had set up a trading post. It was kind of a 7-Eleven of the wilderness. They sold general merchandise and labor and shipped out hides, meat, berries, potatoes and hay. They made a lot of money.

SCOW-SCHOONER AT A PETALUMA FEED MILL

In 1851, new folks began arriving in Petaluma with such things as seedlings, hogs, cattle, chickens and plows. Garret Keller had built a warehouse on Water Street to facilitate creek traffic and he soon added a bunkhouse and eatery.

James Hudspeth built another warehouse at the foot of Washington Street. Agricultural products flooded in and Petaluma Creek became crowded with scow schooners.

A year later, Keller laid out the plan of a town of 40 acres around this shipping point. That accelerated the activity. A grocery was built. Flogdell and Bayliss built a hotel (The Pioneer). William Zartman, John Fritsch and James Reid built the first blacksmith shop (they later added a carriage factory and livery to it).

The town's population was almost entirely single men and they missed their families from back home. Petaluma was no place for families, though. In 1852, sanitation and hygiene were not good here. Garbage was just thrown anywhere. There were no sewers, no penicillin, no Walgreens. Doctors were almost totally unskilled. Boils, broken bones, scrapes and burns could kill you. Cholera was the biggest killer, but close behind were drowning and gun and horse accidents. Bandages, liniment and disinfectant were hard to come by. Just pouring whiskey in a wound helped, but it sure hurt a lot. Indian poultices of cow dung and moss weren't a lot of fun either. It was a tough life.

Petaluma was still a frontier town. The streets were deep with mud and sidewalks were wooden

The structure was built on the river's edge as a fireproof warehouse with two-foot-thick walls of stone.

EARLY MILL ON THE RIVER

HARRISON MECHAM

planks. Drinking water was brought in by barrel wagons. Most roofs leaked and so did most boats. There were few roads or bridges.

Only 10 years after General Vallejo had completed his headquarters building ("The Old Adobe") and five years after the great gold rush, the Great Petaluma Mill building was begun by the same Thomas Bayliss who had camped on the deserted banks of the Petaluma River just three years earlier. The structure was built on the river's edge as a fireproof warehouse with two-foot-thick walls of stone. It was, by far, the most imposing building for miles around.

The first steamer, "The Red Jacket", plied her way to Petaluma from San Francisco in November 1852. The fare was six dollars. The countryside was still thickly covered with splendid timber, most of which found its way to Petaluma, and commerce became greater each month. Soon, the Petaluma Line of Packets running to San Francisco, Sacramento, and Stockton consisted of the schooners "Petaluma", "Enterprise", and "Blue Wing" and the sloops "Cleopatra", "Star of the West", and "Ned Beale". The ever-present Tom Bayliss was listed as pilot of the schooner "Petaluma". These vessels shipped hay, grain, and livestock and brought back such basic needs as Epsom salts, McGuffy's readers, and hair oils.

Petaluma had become the main shipping depot for Sonoma, Napa and Mendocino Counties. Butter, cheese, eggs, hay, potatoes and wood had replaced wild game as the main exports. In fact, Petaluma had become the depot and outlet for the farming interests of the surrounding country as far north as Clear Lake. The wealth of the area had shifted to agriculture, but it was all based on the ability to ship on Petaluma Creek.

Petaluma's population had grown to nearly 1,200, but the people were spread over a wide area. There were less than 50 real houses (of clapboard or slats) and half of those had dirt floors. Then, a man named Harrison Mecham — who had hit it big in the gold fields — bought a vast piece of land stretching from Washoe House to Two Rock and stocked it with a thousand cattle. Also that year, a stage line was started between Petaluma and Sonoma.

By 1855, the first newspaper — *The Petaluma Weekly Journal and Sonoma County Advertiser* — had begun publication. City government was right around the corner. It would mean fewer freedoms and some begrudged the loss. Imagine Bayliss, Flogdell and Lockwood looking out upon a paradise loaded with game and great prospects — with no taxes, fences or ordinances to hold them back. It must have been incredible.

Petaluma was granted a town charter in 1858. Ordinances were passed that year against permitting hogs and goats to roam at large within the city limits. There were also public outcries concerning "disorderly conduct, the suppression of houses of ill fame, and the storage of gun powder." Elegant brick and stone buildings were springing up and some of the muddy roads had been graded and cobble-stoned. In 1860, the city was officially surveyed by W. A. Eliason. Large dairy ranches surrounded Petaluma — including Ezekial Denman's, which was over 4,000 acres. That same year, a petition was made by the residents of Marin County to extend the county line north so that the "boomtown, Petaluma" could become the county seat of Marin. The state legislature voted the plan down.

Petaluma took a great leap forward in four astounding years — from 1862 to 1865.

The Board of Trustees in 1862 was chaired by W. D. Bliss. Also on the Board were such pioneer names as B. F. Tuttle, Samuel Brown, Josiah Chandler, John Cavanagh and F. D. Colton.

One of the early issues confronting this board was the hazardous condition of the silted-in Petaluma Creek. Mr. M. R. Minturn had promptly set up a stream dredge to deepen the creek and he was doing this without public funds. Why? He proposed to dredge only to a spot south of the town called "Italian Garden" where he would place the main steamer landing. He figured that would be a nifty way to take business away from downtown Petaluma and grab it for himself.

At about the same time, the Board of Trustees was approached by William Kohl. Kohl proposed laying down a railroad track with cars drawn by mules from "Italian Garden" to Petaluma. Kohl himself would finance the venture. Before the Board of Trustees could approve either of these projects, the people of Petaluma jumped up and said, "No way!"

MCNEAR MILL WITH SCOW-SCHOONER AT THE DOCK IN THE BACKGROUND

Petaluma as a community was prospering wildly. Real estate sales were brisk.
Wood shanties gave way to substantial buildings.

Also in 1862, the city imposed a license tax on billiard tables and "dram" shops. Cigars, however, were still a nickel and remained untaxed for many years.

Petaluma as a community was prospering wildly. Real estate sales were brisk. Wood shanties gave way to substantial buildings. Here you could find the blacksmith shop of William Ordway, the tannery of Mr. Baily, the carriage works of Fritsch & Zartman, the foundry of Hatch & Cobb, and the match factory of Mr. Hutchings. There were few unoccupied houses and many being built. The streets were crowded with wagons and buggies. The wharves were alive with schooners, barges, and longshoremen. Agriculture was pouring in from Napa and Mendocino Counties for shipping to San Francisco and beyond. Buildings were springing up all around. It was a place of great energy and unprecedented growth.

In May of 1863, a law was passed allowing C. M. Baxter to erect a gas works and lay pipes through the city streets. On the evening of December 19, 1863, the city of Petaluma was lit by gas lamps. An ordinance was also passed prohibiting the blowing of steam whistles within the city limits. Too many horses and babies were being frightened.

The school census of 1863 was 270 males and 251 females under 18. Quite a crop for a new town.

One of the most talked-about events in these years was the purchase of the old Vigilante Bell from San Francisco. Several locals bought it and had it brought to Petaluma — all for less than $700. M. Doyle was one of those who hoisted it to the belfry of the First Baptist Church. The conditions on the deal, however, were that it would be used by the city on "all occasions when bells are usually in requisition." The city had to keep a man employed at all hours in case ringing the bell became necessary.

This became a big, nasty problem during the Civil War.

MR. AND MRS. WILLIAM WISEMAN
POSE WITH THE VIGILANTE BELL

© PETALUMA MUSEUM ASSOCIATION

No, California and Petaluma did not escape the war. Volunteer regiments were sent from Petaluma to reinforce the side of "the blues" from the North. Southerners in town took umbrage to the ringing of the Vigilante Bell on the occasion of Yankee victories. The church was split on the issue. Some Southern sympathizers began moving north to Santa Rosa, which was rebel territory. Churches, families and fraternal groups were split because of this terrible war between the states, and a mini war nearly broke out between Santa Rosa and Petaluma. Tempers were short. Mr. Doyle — himself a secessionist — got together a posse, hoisted the bell out and locked it in a warehouse until the public finally demanded it be returned. In the course of all this turmoil, the bell was cracked.

But the killing of a man who was finally bringing the country to peace froze nearly everyone's emotions. 1865 was the fateful year of the assassination of Abraham Lincoln. The Petaluma Board of Trustees issued this proclamation: "We are called upon to mourn the decease of our honored Chief Magistrate, stricken down by the hand of an assassin, in the height of his power and usefulness and at a time when all manly hearts yearned for a speedy restoration of peace. In our land, therefore, be it resolved that we regard the death of Abraham Lincoln, a great national calamity."

April 14, 1865, was a national day of mourning. The board of trustees of Petaluma resolved that citizens wear black crepe for 30 days. Stores were closed, church bells rang a slow cadence, and Petaluma turned out en masse for a special funeral service given by Professor E. S. Lippett in Walnut Park. The last of Professor Lippett's words were, "The history of his life and the story of his death will be assigned a place in the world's archives." Of course, he was right.

Later that year, the city assigned a contract to improve Petaluma Creek for navigation. At that same meeting, it was resolved by the trustees to "conclude the

LEFT: MAIN STREET IN THE LATE 1800S (NOTE THE FAINT IMAGE OF A TIGHTROPE WALKER CROSSING AT ROOFTOP LEVEL UPPER LEFT)

procedures early so that all desirous of doing so may attend the lecture of one Mark Twain." The town was also privileged to receive such entertainers as Tom Thumb and Emperor Norton.

In 1866, a railroad company was formed to connect Petaluma to Healdsburg. William P. Hill was appointed treasurer and directors were H. Mecham, P. E. Weeks, William Zartman, J. S. Van Doren, A. P. Whitney, Alex McCune, and Thomas Hopper. William Hill's son, Alexander, was to marry into the Fairbanks family, and the Golden Eagle Milling Company, which was founded by Fairbanks, soon moved into the competent hands of the Hills.

It was not until 1870, however, that Peter Donahue of the North Pacific Railroad Company was finally able to get the Iron Horse running into Petaluma. Donahue, as part of the deal for the right to run the railroad, purchased the gas works and supplied downtown gaslights to the city at no cost.

By now, Petaluma was really booming. In 1870, it had three tanneries, one undertaker, two flour mills, 11 blacksmiths, one gunsmith and a boot shop. There were also seven hotels, the Petaluma Theater, four tobacco stores, two breweries, seven livery stables, and 27 billiard and saloon parlors (featuring, upstairs, the inevitable ladies of ill repute).

The population of the United States in 1876 had grown to 43 million and it was the centennial of our country. It was also in 1876 that the Sioux nation wiped out Lieutenant Colonel George Custer on the Little Big Horn. It was their last hurrah. Three million buffalo were being senselessly slaughtered each year and Sitting Bull, the great Sioux leader, became a fugitive in Canada. For the American Indian, the world had sadly changed.

The country was fairly boiling with expansion and new ideas. Oil had been discovered in Pennsylvania. Railroads were expanding to every corner of the nation. The telephone had been invented and steel plants had sprung up all over the East. Lackluster Republican Rutherford B. Hayes had won the presidency by a bare whisker over Samuel Tilden, but the Industrial Revolution had its beginnings in spite of him. Merchant princes and mechanical geniuses were creating the excitement, but much of it was still fed by the nation's flourishing agriculture.

Through the 1870s, cattle drives were underway across vast unoccupied grasslands of the West — but in 1874, barbed wire was invented, windmills developed, and John Deere told the world he had a new kind of plow. The farm began to edge out the ranch and the West began to change. Petaluma was in the forefront of this agricultural change and had, by now, become the number one depot of agricultural exchange and trade for 50 miles in all directions.

By 1877, Petaluma already had three churches (Methodist, Episcopalian and Congregational). It had four benevolent societies (Masons, I.O.O.F, Turn Verein Hibernians and the Mutual Relief Association). It had an excellent library and a great fire department, "which had proven its prowess in many hard fought battles," and retail and manufacturing were also bustling along. We had seven lawyers and twelve saloons. Imagine that! More saloons than lawyers!

The most important industry next to agriculture was the manufacture of buggies and wagons. In 1877, more than 245 carriages were made in Petaluma. More than 500 sets of harnesses and 500 saddles were also made here that year.

There were nine boot makers in Petaluma. All those shoes, saddles, and harnesses were made because of the booming cattle business here. Petaluma was where the cowhide was.

There were four tinshops here. Why four tinshops? The answer again is the dairies, which needed storage containers and milk cans and more. There were also two breweries in Petaluma and, together, they produced an astonishing 81,000 gallons of beer. Barley and hops were grown in great plenty in this area.

Soon, L. C. Byce would invent the Petaluma Egg Incubator and many of the city's residents would learn that there was good profit in the raising of chickens and the sale of eggs. L. C. Byce and the Feed Barons were to become very wealthy. Unknown to them, the town was one day to become the "Egg Basket of the World." This industry would become so important that, by 1915, more dollars per capita were on deposit in Petaluma banks than in any other city in the United States.

The Great Petaluma Mill Building, constructed by Thomas Baylis in 1854 — and variously known as the Golden Eagle Milling Company, the McNear Mill (the famous G. P. McNear) and the Wickersham Warehouse — still stands as a monument to the thriving agricultural base of this town. Its "products" are vastly different now, but "The Mill" is still here, its thick stone walls untouched by earthquakes or any other disaster. In 1975, The Mill was destined for demolition. Fortunately, the oldest standing commercial structure in Petaluma has been preserved

The most important industry next to agriculture was the manufacture of buggies and wagons. In 1877, more than 245 carriages were made in Petaluma. More than 500 sets of harnesses and 500 saddles were also made here that year.

and has become the current home of retail shops, offices, restaurants and the 24-Hour Fitness facility.

In many ways, the early settlers came to Petaluma for the same reasons new arrivals do today. I felt a terrific thrill myself in 1957 when I first came to California. Rather than a covered wagon, I had arrived in a Chrysler with air conditioning and I had not suffered the ills of a six-month trip. But imagine how the Petaluma Valley must have seemed to those who had traversed the Great Plains, mountains, and deserts to get to Sonoma County. Here are some quotes from the 1800s:

In 1880, one lad wrote, "The average rainfall here is perfect. We have never lost a crop to drought. It commences to rain in October and ends in May. As soon as it rains, the hills turn green and the cattle feed."

"Even in December, it seldom goes as low as 37 degrees above zero and in late January, the almond trees blossom and the robins come," wrote a young girl home to her grandma in Missouri. "Grain may be sown in January, February or March and it will produce well." Can you imagine what that meant to a farmer from the Midwest or East?

After the rainy season, the farmers found that the crops were still watered by fogs and first harvest was ready by late July. It seemed as if each year produced a good crop — 80 to 100 bushels of wheat per acre mostly — because of the July and August fogs.

"The fog spreads through the county late in the afternoon, continues through the night and disappears after sunrise. We estimate that three heavy fogs equal about a light rain."

"The grass keeps green longer and this helps the productiveness of the dairy cows and the length of the wool on the sheep."

"There seems to be no extreme of heat or cold here. It is probable that more roses bloom in this county than in all the hot houses of New England!" This kind of enthusiastic letter home was a terrific advertisement and more and more settlers came out to see the golden land.

"The same clothing may be worn here all the year around," wrote a young lad. (Of course, that was before Nordstrom.)

"There seems to be a warm strata of air in the hills, a few hundred feet above the valleys. Here, oranges, lemons, limes, English walnuts, almond and pomegranate trees grow well. And, there are thousands of acres of this kind of land in Sonoma County which can be bought for $15 to $20 per acre."

"Sonoma County has an immense source of wealth in its timber. The great redwood, fed by alluvial soil grows to a prodigious size," wrote a young lad to his lumberjack father in Virginia. Going on, he said, "They grow in some cases to over 350 feet and have a diameter of 15 feet. It is said that just one of these trees can produce 65,000 feet of lumber worth at least a thousand dollars!"

The redwood, of course, needs fog. It is a close-grained timber that splits and saws well and does not warp or shrink — a most durable asset. The loggers flooded in. Towns like Occidental became "company towns," where many lived full-time until all the trees were gone — and those in company towns "owed their souls to the company stores."

Today, the fog contributes to the quality of the grapes grown in the Petaluma Gap and to the quality of the wines made from them. The climate also provides wonderful conditions for growing vegetables and raising dairy cattle, sheep and goats. These, in turn, provide ingredients for some of the finest cuisine in the country. New residents and tourists alike are drawn here by the restaurants, the galleries and antique shops, and the small town way of life Petaluma has managed to preserve, despite its growth. This is still a wonderful place to visit, to work and to live.

FOUR

FROM LONGHORNS TO DAIRY CATTLE
by Skip Sommer

The real wave of cowboys moving west came with the cattle drives from Texas, filling the orders of men like Harrison Mecham.

People came west
because they wanted more — more adventure, more freedom, more land, more opportunity, more of everything. The excitement of discovery was contagious. In 1849 and 1850, men came from all over the world to try their luck at finding California gold. It was one of the largest mass movements of population in world history. Within three years, though, the surface gold was gone and most miners either returned home or — if they had the right skills and vision — continued farther westward from the gold fields. Some "49ers" had been wildly successful and brought gold to the Petaluma Valley to purchase land.

Harrison Mecham was one of those who had hit it big in the gold fields. He bought a vast parcel of land stretching from the Washoe House to Two Rock and made a very important decision: he would stock his ranch with longhorn cattle from Texas. Mecham was a wealthy and cautious man. It was said that he never rode or drove anywhere without "outrider" guards. His decision for longhorns was to greatly affect our community.

The population was 97% male, and most of the men were misfits who could not live by society's rules. Many had hired on as guards for the wagon trains crossing the plains. If they had a horse and could shoot, they were given food and protected by the size of the wagon train as they crossed the wilderness. These men were the first cowboys in the Petaluma Valley.

Those first cowboys did not get much practice with their weapons because bullets were so expensive and hard to come by. Anyway, many

of them had just purchased their first guns in Missouri and faked prowess to get into a wagon train going to the gold fields.

The real wave of cowboys moving west came with the cattle drives from Texas, filling the orders of men like Harrison Mecham. Herds of 500 to 3,000 longhorns required a lot of attention from a lot of horsemen. The movies and television have fantasized this era beyond recognition. Cattle were, indeed, "king" from 1850 through 1880, but driving a herd across the plains and the Sierras was not at all glamorous. It was perilous, dusty, and incredibly hard work. The men known as "cowboys" had to be young, tough, and gutsy.

In 1858, when Petaluma officially became a town, there were 3,588 longhorn cattle in Sonoma County — most of them in the Petaluma Valley. Supplies were still brought in by mule and ox teams. Mail came in once a week by horseback. Wild bear, elk, and deer were prevalent here and you really could live off the land.

DAVID JENSEN

Milk cows, however, survived. The word "milk" comes from the early English word "milch," which meant "a source of easily acquired gain." Ranchers made sure these milk cows made it through the drought, but I'm pretty sure it wasn't "easily."

Sadly the longhorns, needing a constant supply of grass for feed, vanished with the big drought of 1862-1864. Milk cows, however, survived. The word "milk" comes from the early English word "milch", which meant "a source of easily acquired gain." Ranchers made sure these milk cows made it through the drought, but I'm pretty sure it wasn't "easily." In 1858, there were more than 5,000 milk cows in Sonoma County and many more in Marin. The milk was home-processed into butter or cheese. The butter was heavily salted for preservation and packed into barrels for cellar storage. It could last all winter, although it probably tasted kind of funny in the spring.

Freighters put in once a week at Petaluma, and also at Tomales, for butter shipments. Most of the butter was sent down to San Francisco, but much was also shipped to other ports. In 1870, butter shipments still far exceeded those of eggs. The butter was shipped in 110-pound barrels. About 186,000 pounds were shipped in 1869, along with 1,600 pounds of cheese. Combined with the fast growing egg and grain business, Petaluma's agricultural commerce was bustling. It went out by mule team and horse and wagon, as well as on the scow schooners. River travel was cheap and that was important.

By 1880, Petaluma had become the largest shipping point for dairy products in the State of California. Petaluma's population had grown to 6,000 and the streets were so busy that the city ordered lighting to be placed on the Washington Street Bridge to handle the night wagon traffic. Livery stables took care of horses, carriages, and harnesses for $15 per month. Petaluma's eleven blacksmith and wagon shops were extremely busy also. Zartman's Carriage Works turned out as many as 100 buggies a year. D. W. C. Putnam's patented horse cart was very popular, and Robinson & Farrel's Carriage Emporium was successful enough to propel William Farrel into the position of Mayor. Farrel purchased a very fine home on Washington Street. The house was moved to Weller Street overlooking the Turning Basin some years ago and it's now The River House.

Supplemental feeding, in the dairy business, was going full blast in 1895. That meant more and bigger feed mills with better scientific methods, especially for the new purebred cattle — Guernseys, Jerseys, Holsteins, Ayrshires and Brown Swiss. Production went up. Quality went up. New distribution facilities had to be created. The Petaluma Cooperative Creamery and the Western Condensing Company

were two of these. "The Co-op" is now Spring Hill Jersey Cheese on Western Avenue.

With the chicken industry ramping up, even more feed mills were needed. Hunt & Behrens, Vonson's, Barlas, and Shelling were some of the new mills coming into the community at this time. Vonson's later became Bar-Ale, on the corner of First and D Streets by the bridge. Barlas, Shelling, and Hunt & Behrens are still here, too. The dairies, the horse and cattle breeding, the chickens, the fields of grain and grass, the fruit trees and the grapes all flourished. The early pioneers had been right. Our climate and soil would produce an abundance of fine agricultural produce.

One early settler to recognize the potential in the dairy business was an Italian-Swiss immigrant, Battista Gambonini. In 1868, he traveled by ship to Panama. Then he rode on a flatcar across the isthmus and proceeded again by ship to San Francisco. It was a grueling trip of 46 days. The flatcar across hot tropical Panama was an invitation to cholera and diphtheria. Many of his traveling companions, already weakened by a rough sea voyage from New York, did not make it. Battista did. He spoke no English and had little money when he arrived.

In Petaluma, Battista found work on the Brown ranch in Hicks Valley. He would work nine years as a ranch hand before he was able to lease his own ranch (now known as Rancho Nicasio in Marin). Battista was ecstatic about the opportunities the new state offered him. In 1879, he married Maria Maggini. She was 16. He was 33. Battista continued renting ranches until 1908, when he was able to purchase part of the LeBaron ranch near Bodega Bay.

Paulo Dado had also come over from Switzerland. He arrived in California in 1864. Like Gambonini, Dado had little money and could speak no English — but, by 1871, he had saved enough to purchase 497 acres in Tomales adjoining the Gamboninis' piece. Paulo returned to Switzerland to marry Carolina Togni in 1874. He brought her back to California, where they had 11 children.

Paulo Dado and Battista Gambonini met repairing fence lines in March of 1894. They both exclaimed that their wives had borne a child that same morning. "Would it be possible that my son Silvio should marry your daughter Evelina and join our families some day?" wondered Battista.

THE WEDDING OF SILVIO GAMBONINI AND EVELINA DADO, 1909

PAULO AND CAROLINE DADO (CENTER RIGHT) AND ELEVEN CHILDREN IN 1918

Twenty-seven years later, in 1909 — after spending childhood and school days together — Silvio and Evelina did marry. Life in the Dado and Gambonini families was a happy and boisterous one. When Paulo or Battista went to San Francisco, they brought back Ghirardelli chocolate for all and bags of shoes from Chinatown to fit all sizes. The children would walk across the poppy fields to school in "Portuguese Beach" with the Cheda and Bolla kids. At recess, they played on the sandy beach. When it stormed, one of the parents would drive out to pick them up in a six-seat buggy with the curtains rolled down.

The cows were milked outdoors by hand — rain or shine — at 4 a.m. and 4 p.m. every day. Each hand was responsible for 1,525 cows. Wages were $30 per month (plus room and board) and they were paid at the end of the season. The season was set by the availability of natural pasture and pretty much slowed down by October.

Hoppers, strainers, holding tanks, paddles, churns, and butter molds were made in Petaluma by local tinsmiths and carpenters. Milk was poured into hoppers, strained, and placed on trays for 48 hours. It was then skimmed and the skim milk was dumped into chutes that went right to the hog pens. The cream went into the churns to become butter.

The whole family helped with the separating and churning, which was all done by hand. Then the butter was heavily salted and packed in boxes with the maker's mark burned in.

Butter was sold to merchants in San Francisco, who charged a commission of five percent. Sometimes Battista and Paulo would take their butter all the way to San Francisco. Sometimes they would consign it to the schooners Red Jacket, E. Corning and Mary C., which made regular round trips. Cost was $6 each way and it was an all-day sail.

Every two weeks, the Gamboninis and Dados would bring their butter to town by horse and wagon. If the weather was good, the two families would often picnic by the river and watch the boats. After that, there were trips to various shops for provisions.

Gradually, dairies became larger and more efficient. By 1880, Petaluma was the largest shipping point for dairy products in the state. Thirty scow schooners were working the creek and more than 12,000 tons of butter were shipped that year.

By 1877, Petaluma was well established as the "dairy and egg" capital of California. That year, 3,500,000 pounds of butter, 750,000 pounds of cheese, 75,000 dozen eggs and 12,000 calves were shipped from this small city.

The invention of the milk bottle in 1884 made handling and distribution of milk easier — and pasteurization was a big leap forward in terms of sanitation. In 1894, the milk separator was invented and very soon every dairy had one. By 1905, the average dairy herd in

Sonoma County had grown to 50 and small creameries were joining into large co-ops.

Silvio and Evelina Gambonini bought a big ranch on Lakeville in 1914. They had four children. One of them — Earl — married Esther Giacomini in 1936. Earl took over the dairy in 1947. Their son George married Margaret Gervasoni in 1962. George and Margaret's dairy, Gam Lake, was named outstanding dairy of the year in 1989. Frank Gambonini — the great, great-grandson of Battista — became a partner in the dairy in 1993. He and his wife, Stacey, continue to manage the Gam Lake dairy successfully. In 2007, Margaret Gambonini was awarded The Community Recognition Award for Excellence in Agriculture.

LINDA SUGAR

Natural Selection

BILLBOARD ART COURTESY CLOVER STORNETTA FARMS

EDITOR'S NOTE

Looking to the future, much has been written about the difficulty family dairies will have competing with the vastly larger operations such as those in California's Central Valley — some with herds of as many as 10,000 cows. The answer may be in a different approach to the market.

Clover Stornetta, among others, has made a commitment to sustainable agriculture. There is no added rBST in any of their products. Clover takes pride in its "Free Farmed" certification by the American Humane Association and guarantees knowledge of where 100 percent of their milk comes from every day. With the FDA close to a ruling in favor of the use of cloned cows for milk

and meat, Clover has said it won't accept milk from cloned cows.

Straus Family Creamery also opposes clones and positions itself as "a small family-owned organic dairy and creamery" where all products are produced organically, in small batches. Albert Straus admits their processes are not as efficient as those in "big plants," but he believes consumers appreciate the difference in taste and quality.

It would seem that they do. It would seem that Bay Area consumers, in particular, appreciate both the products and the message behind them — support of family farms and environmentally friendly practices. They will even pay a little more.

FIVE

PETALUMA TRAINS — HORSE, STEAM & ELECTRIC
by Vangie Pullins

"On a train,
all things are possible."

Paul Theroux (b. 1941), American novelist.

SCOTT HESS

RESTORED RAILWAY EXPRESS BUILDING

Trains today

have a drastically smaller presence in our American cultural landscape than they did a century ago. In the railroad's heyday, trains directly touched the lives of most citizens. This was certainly the case in Petaluma.

Today the train depot is located near the heart of the city, on Lakeville Highway between East Washington and D Street, and includes three buildings dating to 1914. The depot is a Spanish-revival structure with a tile roof and stucco walls, leased by the City of Petaluma and renovated. It now houses the Petaluma Visitor Center. The buildings and land are owned by the *Northwestern Pacific Railroad Authority*.

But this was not the location of the first railroad depot in Petaluma. To begin writing about the history of Petaluma's trains and depot, one must start with the Petaluma Creek (as it was called then). The Petaluma Creek was not upgraded to "River" status until an Act of Congress was signed by President Eisenhower on June 16, 1959.

Commercial use of the Petaluma Creek began more than a century earlier, in the summer of 1851. By 1852, the captains navigating its twists and turns and shallow waters had discovered they could travel as far into town as Haystack Landing (also known as Rudesill's). It is said that Haystack Landing was so named because of a group of haystacks left to molder there all winter in the 1840s. Haystack Landing was about three miles below town, just below today's southernmost Petaluma freeway exit, and not far from the marina. From there, travelers and goods had to be unloaded and brought into Petaluma by horse and wagon.

Anywhere that was anywhere in the mid-1800s had a steam railway. Petaluma's very first train was the *Petaluma and Haystack Railroad*, a steam-driven train. It was the third rail line built in California and — though credit is given to Charles Minturn — the idea was actually hatched in 1864 by Captain Thomas Fulsher Baylis. Baylis planned to modernize Petaluma's transportation with a horse-drawn railroad. The first such passenger line in city streets — in the world, in fact — to use horse-drawn cars was the *New York & Harlem* in 1832. Baylis felt it was time for Petaluma to get modern. With his railroad, steamboat travelers and goods would be able to travel by rail from Haystack Landing into town, greatly expanding his own commercial enterprises on the river.

In the early days of steamboat trade on the river, there was fierce competition between the major players — Tom Baylis, Charles Minturn, and John A. McNear. The competition escalated when Baylis formed a corporation to build a horse-drawn railroad from Petaluma to Haystack Landing. Petaluma citizens opposed his project, however, on the grounds that Baylis and his partners would have a monopoly.

In the end, however, Charles Minturn wound up with an equally monopolistic franchise. He opened the *Petaluma & Haystack Railroad* for business on August 1, 1864. Minturn used steam instead of horses

and mules. His train ran along the west bank of the creek from Haystack Landing into town, a distance of more than two miles. The train had four passenger cars and an Atlas 26-horsepower locomotive. Known as the "Ferryboat King" of San Francisco Bay and detested by Petalumans, Minturn built no wagon road along the tracks. The only way to get back and forth between Minturn's steamers and Petaluma was to ride Minturn's railroad. But Minturn didn't entirely get his way. He petitioned that the downtown plaza (located at Petaluma Boulevard and B Street today) be set aside for a depot. The plan was opposed by Tom Baylis and many others. Minturn had to settle for a plot on the southeast corner of 2nd and B Streets instead, and he wasn't happy about it. Sometimes he charged outrageous fees, and his railcars were poorly maintained. Still, Minturn's steam train operated until his engine exploded at the depot in 1866. After that, his train was converted to horse-drawn, as originally planned by Baylis.

A Horse-drawn Railroad

The explosion of Minturn's steam locomotive on August 27, 1866, led to the conversion from steam to horse-power. Minturn was known for cutting corners to save money, and on that day a former tugboat engineer named John Levitt temporarily filled in as the fireman as well as the engineer. The pilot of the steamboat *Petaluma*, Captain

Warner, often also acted as the conductor of the train. Sixty or seventy passengers boarded at the depot for the ride to the steamboats at Haystack Landing. Levitt blew the whistle to signal departure, and the high-pitched sound caused bystanders to back off. One of them, though, heard Levitt say there was no water in the tank. He likely didn't know that, as fireman, filling the tank was his job. Within minutes the locomotive burst into pieces. Boiler fragments flew in all directions. One chunk weighing several hundred pounds landed a block away at Main and B Street. Levitt and many passengers died. Among those with minor injuries was John McNear, who claimed his life was spared because his shoelace came loose and he ducked down to tie it. Most of the passengers had already boarded the cars so they were protected from the blast. When the dead and injured had been removed, the rest of the passengers were taken to the landing by horse-drawn coach. A grand jury investigation concluded that Levitt had temporarily gone mad at the controls — and Minturn never had to shoulder any responsibility for the tragedy.

Minturn is said to have ordered another locomotive right away, but none ever arrived. For the rest of its eleven-year history, ending in 1875, the railroad cars were pulled by horses and mules. In 1912, the old railroad bed was unearthed at 2nd and B Streets and the redwood ties had been worn almost in half by the shoes of four small mules. It had become a horse-drawn railroad after all.

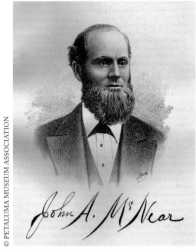

JOHN A. MCNEAR

By the late 1860s, many Petalumans feared that Petaluma would lose upcountry trade to the *Napa Valley Railroad*. Petaluma needed its own steam-driven train to secure its future prosperity. If Petaluma had a train running to Healdsburg, and the creek was dredged to the wharves, Petalumans were certain that their town would become the second most important city in the state, after San Francisco.

In 1865, Isaac Wickersham established Sonoma County's first bank, the I. G. Wickersham Company, on Main Street in Petaluma. Between 1868 and 1870, he, John McNear, and other leaders organized several railroad companies. The problem was that they were dependent on public contributions and kept running out of money. Their dream of a steam-driven railroad failed completely and the townspeople became very discouraged and skeptical of any railroad schemes. Minturn's horse-drawn *Petaluma & Haystack Railroad* was still the only railroad operating in Sonoma County. By then, the steam-driven *California Pacific Railroad* had expanded to include the *Napa Valley Railroad* (one of the railroads organized by Wickersham and McNear), chugging ahead and representing a very real threat to Petaluma's economy.

A Colonel Peter Donahue bought the floundering *Sonoma County Railroad* (another one of the railroads organized by Wickersham's group) on November 17, 1869. Donahue's list of notable accomplishments is endless, including the first street railway in San Francisco. By the late 1860s, stands of redwood close to San Francisco had been cleared, but the virgin forests around the Russian River would be available with railroad access. Within four months, Donahue had trains running to Santa Rosa — and by January 1, 1871, he started regular service from San Francisco to Santa Rosa. Two years later his steam-driven *San Francisco and North Pacific Railroad* (*SF&NP*) extended service to Healdsburg and Cloverdale. A branch line was run from Fulton to Guerneville to bring down the redwood. Originally, Donahue planned to make Petaluma the terminus of the railroad, but when he was refused permission to run his railroad down Main Street (now Petaluma Boulevard), he turned completely against Petaluma. He promptly built his tracks eight miles south of Petaluma. In fact, he built a new town, complete with modern amenities including a luxury hotel, a dancehall and a schoolhouse. He called it Donahue, of course.

Wickersham and many other Petalumans were furious with Peter Donahue — so furious that they ignored their earlier lack of success with railroad-building. In 1872, they held a meeting at the Petaluma Theatre (now the Opera House building at 145 Kentucky Street).

There they organized their own company: the steam driven *Sonoma & Marin Railroad* (*S&M*). The McNears promised an acre of land to each investor who purchased five shares of stock. Many took him up on it. They planned to connect Petaluma with San Rafael. In 1868, John McNear had purchased five miles of waterfront at Point San Pedro (now McNear Point) in San Rafael with dreams of using the land for a railroad. In 1872 they began grading the roadbed through the salt marshes toward Novato. In 1875 the directors of the *S&M* purchased the remains of the horse-drawn *Petaluma & Haystack Railroad* from the late Charles Minturn's company. Once again, however, nothing went right. Income for the first year was just $60,000. Most of it went to pay for grading and tunnel construction. In addition, *S&M* rolling stock consisted solely of a badly-maintained locomotive, a dilapidated passenger car, and a caboose inherited from Minturn's company.

As a result, Donahue was soon able to add the *S&M* and the *Petaluma & Haystack* to his ever-growing *San Francisco & North Pacific Railroad*. In 1877 the *SF&NP* entered San Rafael. Donahue built a railroad swing bridge south of town at the old landing. It proved to be such a problem that it was replaced by the present drawbridge in 1903. The *S&M* affected Donahue's creek business and, although he tried to end its service, he was compelled to keep it in operation. By 1882, though, business at the town of Donahue had dropped to almost nothing. Petalumans were ecstatic, but Donahue wasn't ready to give up. Always practical, he moved his town, one building at a time — by barge — to Tiburon. It stood about a mile below Gilardi's on the Lakeville Highway. Today, in Gilardi's parking lot, at the east corner near the highway, there is a stone monument wall with a hole in it. With your back to Gilardi's, placing your eyes up to the hole, you will see the exact area of land where the town of Donahue once stood. By 1898, the *SF&NP* line running past the old wooden depot in Petaluma had changed its name to the *California Northwestern*. In 1907, it changed again to the *Northwestern Pacific Railroad*.

HORSES AGAIN, IN THE MEANTIME

A new horse-drawn railcar service, the *Petaluma Street Railroad* was incorporated October 14, 1889. Records in 1897 show that its route was from 12th Street via F Street, 6th Street, Liberty Street, Western Avenue, Kentucky Street, Washington Street, across Petaluma Creek and across the *SF&NP Railroad* tracks to just beyond Mary Street, with a branch from Washington Street between Payran and Mary Streets, south into the fairgrounds to a point opposite Jefferson Street. The car barn and stables were located on F Street between 11th and 12th Streets. There were 2.5 miles of 4' 8-1/2" gauge 35-pound T rail, with four cars and four horses. The *Petaluma Street Railroad* was sold in 1900, under foreclosure, to the F. A. Wickersham Banking Company of Petaluma.

ELECTRIC RAILWAYS

Just after the turn of the century, in 1902, the *Santa Rosa Street Railways*, an electric car railway, was formed and acquired three horse-drawn railways: the *Union Street Railway*, the *Central Street Railway*, and the *Santa Rosa Street Railway*. These horse-drawn railways continued to operate under their respective names until 1903.

In June, 1903, the *Petaluma and Santa Rosa Railway* (*P&SR*) was incorporated, to be Petaluma's electric car railway. John McNear was president and Burke Corbet was treasurer. The route was to be from Petaluma north to Santa Rosa and northwest through Green Valley to Forestville. Then, from some convenient point on this line, it would turn southwest to Sebastopol. It would also have lines from Sebastopol to Santa Rosa and Forestville. By September, Burke Corbet was granted a forty-year franchise by the City of Petaluma to construct and operate an electric street railway on Main Street from the northern city limits to Third Street, then along Third Street to the southeast city limits and southeast along First Street to the city limits. The franchise also allowed a route from Petaluma Creek, southeast along Copeland Street, to the tidal basin or wharf. Also in September, the *P&SR* purchased the *Petaluma Street Railroad*, the horse-drawn rail service, owned by the F. A. Wickersham Banking Company of Petaluma. At the same time the *P&SR* purchased the *Santa Rosa Street Railways*. In November, the *P&SR* acquired Corbet's franchise, too, but never used it. These lines were purchased for their franchise rights only, but never operated under the franchises and new ones had to be acquired. *P&SR* indicated that they were going to electrify these lines, but they never did, except on Fourth Street in Santa Rosa.

STEAMER GOLD

The *P&SR* continued to expand.

They bought the stern paddlewheel *Steamer Gold* in December 1903 and had already been traveling daily between Petaluma and San Francisco for several years. (This was Petaluma's first *Gold*, built in 1883 and burned in 1920.) On April 5, 1904, the first spike was driven at the steamer landing at the foot of Copeland Street in Petaluma. A rock crushing plant was erected at the quarry to furnish ballast for the track. *P&SR* was granted franchises during 1904 to construct electric railways on certain streets. The first four passenger cars came from St. Louis, Missouri, and were named *Petaluma*, *Woodworth*, *Sebastopol* and *Santa Rosa*. The cars had won a medal at the St. Louis World's Fair and cost nearly $5,700 each. The first regular electric train schedule began on November 29, 1904, from Petaluma to the steam driven *California Northwestern* (*CNW*) crossing in Santa Rosa. (One must remember the *CNW* rail line in Petaluma had been the Donahue's steam driven *SF&NP* six years earlier.)

GEORGE P. MCNEAR

The president of the *CNW*, A. W. Foster, told *P&SR* that it could not cross their right-of-way on Sebastopol Avenue in Santa Rosa. This was the beginning of a controversy that lasted several months and flared into open warfare at this crossroad. Pages have been written about this battle. From January 3 to March 1, 1905, the *CNW* tried to keep *P&SR* from crossing, and during that time the citizens of Santa Rosa witnessed an ugly physical struggle between the two rail companies that finally ended with a Superior Court restraining order commanding the *CNW* to cease its forcible opposition. At 12:45 a.m. on March 2, 1905, the first interurban electric car rolled through the crossing. Naturally, the *P&SR* ended the horse-drawn car lines.

By now, *P&SR* had three steamboats operating between Petaluma and San Francisco. In 1905, William Cattell was president and John McNear was now vice-president of *P&SR*. Ambitious extensions of the railway were planned with the *Marin Terminal Railroad* and the *Santa Rosa & Northern Railroad*. An extension from Petaluma to Point Pedro near San Rafael, where ferries would have picked up passengers to San Francisco, was under construction when the earthquake on April 18, 1906, rendered resumption of the construction impossible.

THE BEGINNING OF THE END

Various changes in the economy — including the 1906 earthquake, the increasing travel by auto and truck, and the depression in 1929 — all played a role in the downward spiral of the steam and electric railroads serving Petaluma and its neighbors. In 1907, the *P&SR* had 620,219 rail passengers, peaking in 1914 to 757,759. There was a steady decline after that, however, with passenger numbers dropping to 53,586 in mid-1932 when service ended. *P&SR's* steamboats had 8,761 passengers in 1907, dropping dramatically to 1,877 in 1917 and down to 15 passengers in 1935 when their service also ended.

The *Petaluma Transportation Company* began operating on the Petaluma Creek in 1908 and cut into the *P&SR* business to a certain extent, but *PTC* ceased its unprofitable operation by December 1908. The stockholders of the *P&SR Railway* were in a desperate financial situation when they organized the *Petaluma & Santa Rosa Railroad* in 1918. The *P&SR Railroad* purchased the *P&SR Railway* at a foreclosure sale on October 29, 1918. The old company was dissolved

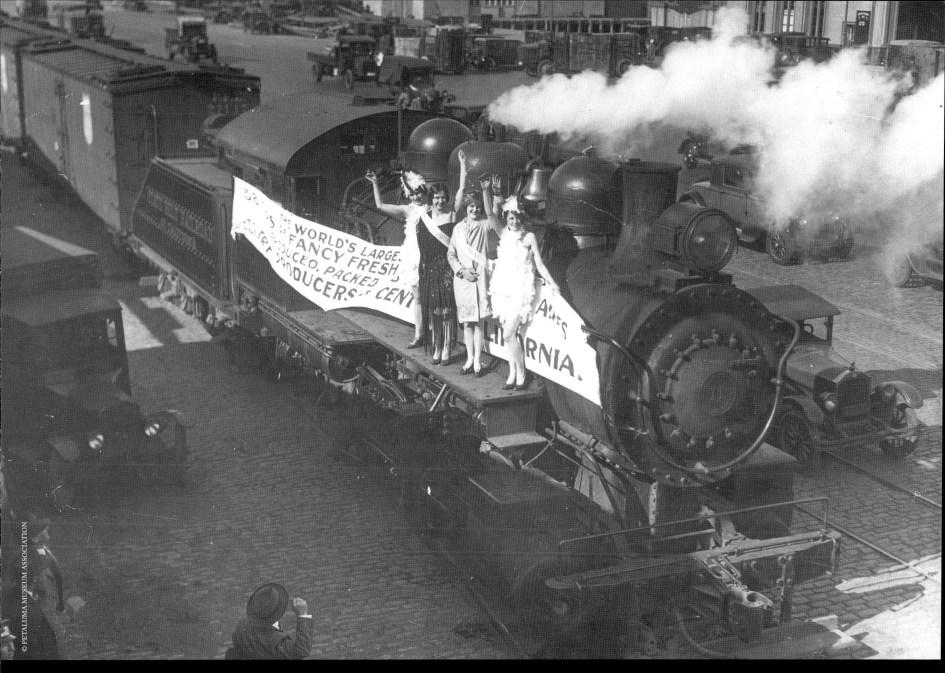

YINGSHI TANG

PETALUMA DEPOT

by December. The new company included Thomas Maclay as president and George McNear (John McNear's son) as vice-president and treasurer.

Almost every city of consequence around the world operated trolley lines, providing cheap, reliable transport for the masses. Petaluma couldn't be any different. Cars were purchased and extensive repairs were made. A franchise was obtained from the City of Petaluma to construct a spur track along the west bank of Petaluma Creek. But the *P&SR Railway's* decline continued.

By the 1920s, automobile manufacturers had begun mass production and reliable motorbuses became available, so it was cheaper to introduce buses that led into the city centers than extend the tracks. Then, on November 8, 1920, the *P&SR's* steamer *Gold* burned while fully loaded at the Petaluma wharf. The wharf itself was destroyed, along with a warehouse and 12 boxcars. That steamer was replaced by the *Fort Bragg,* which was renamed the *Gold*, and the wharf and 10 of the box cars were rebuilt. Work began on the Petaluma Creek west bank spur. That same year, however, the county highway paralleling much of the company's lines was completed, seriously affecting passenger revenue.

In 1927 another war broke out which lasted for several years, although it was not as bloody a battle as was the 1905 affair. It was

a legal battle with the *Northwestern Pacific Railroad* (*NWP*). The depression that started in America in 1929 affected small town streetcar systems and most of them collapsed. Petaluma, again, was no different. The legal battle with the *NWP* ended with that railroad acquiring the *Petaluma & Santa Rosa* stock in 1932. Railroad passenger numbers had dropped so low due to the private auto that all passenger service was discontinued on June 30, 1932 — with passenger service on steamboats ending in 1935. The *Gold* was taken out of service and dismantled in 1940 at Petaluma. It was the end of a long effort by our city's fathers to have their own railroad.

In 1907, the line past the old wooden depot in Petaluma had changed from the *California Northwestern* to the *Northwestern Pacific Railroad*. Thus, the *CNW* came to be owned by the company that also owned the electric railway *CNW* had so vehemently opposed in Santa Rosa. Construction of the steam driven *Northwestern Pacific Railroad* had been completed in 1914. It spanned 314 miles between Schellville, north of San Pablo Bay and Arcata, California. The *NWP* traveled at an average distance of only 30 feet from the Eel and Russian Rivers and Humboldt Bay. In many areas, the track was below the mean water line. It was flooded and wiped out by landslides before it opened and a giant landslide blocked the return of dignitaries to Eureka during the *NWP's* opening event. The new owners brought their own problems to the *P&SR,* but the *NWP* didn't give up. In 1946, two 380 horsepower diesel electric locomotives were purchased to replace the electric operation — as the electric locomotives were in poor condition, obsolete and parts were unavailable, and 75% of the pole lines and trolley wires needed replacement. The plans were to retain the electric operation only in Petaluma. However, on May 31, 1947, the Petaluma line was also discontinued. The last of the trolley wires were taken down on May 31, 1947. The *NWP* came to be owned by *Southern Pacific & Santa Fe Railroad* (*SP&SF*) from the 1950s to the mid-1980s.

The *Southern Pacific & Santa Fe Railroad* was purchased in 1984 by Bryan Wipple, a Eureka businessman. Two years later, Wipple filed for bankruptcy. The Willits-to-Arcata portion of the line remained under a court-appointed trustee until 1992, when the State of California formed the *North Coast Railroad Authority* (*NCRA*) to purchase and manage

the *NWP*. The *NCRA* purchased the entire line from Sonoma County to Arcata. In following years, the track suffered extensive damage and was finally officially closed by the Federal Railroad Authority in 1998. The *Northwestern Pacific Railroad*, also known as *North Coast Railroad Authority*, was terminated effective February 23, 1998.

Today, the trestle built in 1918 by the *Petaluma & Santa Rosa Railroad*, George McNear, and others along the west bank of the river — and the tracks and depot on Lakeville — are all the physical structure that's left of Petaluma's railroad history. Occasionally a freight train travels by the depot, but we cannot walk along the trestle by the river because of the danger of collapse. It is a problem passed down for our city's managers to deal with today. Petaluma's past is rich with history surrounding the railroad and depot. It will be interesting to see what the future brings.

IS THERE A TROLLEY IN OUR FUTURE? THE TROLLEY FROM PETALUMA TO SANTA ROSA, SEBASTOPOL AND FORESTVILLE WAS ONCE ONE OF THE BUSIEST LITTLE RAILROADS IN AMERICA. IT HAULED UP TO 10,000 CARLOADS OF PRODUCE AND PRODUCTS AND A QUARTER OF A MILLION PASSENGERS EACH YEAR. THE INCREASED COMMERCE ENABLED PETALUMA TO CONSTRUCT MANY OF THE BUILDINGS WE TREASURE TODAY. THE TROLLEY SERVICE THAT WAS SO IMPORTANT TO THE PAST COULD BECOME VALUABLE TO US AGAIN. THE FRIENDS OF THE WATER STREET TRESTLE ARE WORKING TO RESTORE THE RIVERSIDE STRUCTURE AND BEGIN LIGHT RAIL TROLLEY SERVICE BETWEEN THE PETALUMA PREMIUM OUTLET MALL AND FOUNDRY WHARF.

SIX

PETALUMA LANDMARKS
by Marianne Hurley and Katherine J. Rinehart with assistance from Lucy Kortum

From its humble beginnings as a hunting camp, Petaluma quickly developed into the hub of commerce and transportation for the surrounding fertile agricultural region.

PETALUMA CITY
HALL, 1943

BRAINERD JONES

From its humble beginnings as a hunting camp, Petaluma quickly developed into the hub of commerce and transportation for the surrounding fertile

agricultural region. Sited at the head of navigation along the Petaluma River, the town prospered with its ability to ship grain, potatoes, poultry, dairy products, fruit, and other local products to San Francisco. Today, two large grain elevators stand as landmarks to the importance agriculture has played in the town's history.

After several decades of growth, the town developed into a sophisticated settlement, complete with ornate cast iron commercial buildings downtown, industrial warehouses, factories along the river and refined residential neighborhoods. The Newsom Brothers from San Francisco designed the handsome 1886 City Hall that unfortunately no longer stands. However, despite efforts to remove some historic builldings, Petaluma retains excellent examples of its

commercial, residential, industrial, and agricultural architecture — some of which are depicted in the following pages.

Much of the town's personality and marketing revolves around its historic position as a major poultry center. In 1879, Lyman Byce and Isaac Dias invented the first practical incubator. A few years later, the first commercial hatchery was established here by Christopher Nisson, laying the foundation for Petaluma's claim as the "Egg Basket of the World."

The dairy industry was equally central to Petaluma's growth and prosperity. Dairy products were an important California and Sonoma County export. By 1880, 76 percent of California's milk, 12 percent of its cheese and nearly 8 percent of its butter were coming from Sonoma County. Much of that was shipped from Petaluma dairies down the Petaluma River to San Francisco and beyond.

Along with the chicken ranches and dairies came the need for supporting businesses such as hatcheries, feed stores, creameries and even a chicken pharmacy. Business expansion created new jobs, a demand for housing and increased wealth for Petaluma. Evidence of these prosperous times is reflected in the splendid architecture found throughout Petaluma.

In the 1950s, Petaluma's economy and demographics began to change. By 1964, a major poultry co-op went bankrupt and the contribution of agriculture to the town's economy receded. Instead, subdivisions began to sprout in the fields east of the freeway, ready for an influx of new residents who worked in San Francisco or Marin. When uncontrolled growth led to a population of 30,000 in 1975, it precipitated a community protest. The courts upheld "The Petaluma Plan" which limited development to 500 units for a five-year period.

Much of Petaluma's architectural distinction is attributed to one of it most creative and productive architects, Brainerd Jones (1869–1945), who was responsible for a large number of the historic buildings found around town today. Jones, a native son, apprenticed with and later worked for McDougall Brothers in San Francisco before starting his own practice in Petaluma in 1900.

Also represented among the town's architectural landmarks are works by William Curlett, Walter J. Cuthbertson, William Henry Weeks, Thomas J. Welsh, Charles Havens, Ernest Coxhead, Leo J. Devlin, Julia Morgan, Albert Farr and several other California architects. It's important to note, however, that a number of Petaluma's architectural treasures are not the products of trained architects, but were designed by local contractors such as O.B. Ackerman, Samuel Rodd, Ed Hedges and D.B. Franklin in the 19th century, and H.P. Vogensen, Walter Singleton, A.M. Seeburg, Clark Trendall, R.W. Moller and William Haskins in the early- to mid- 20th century.

Petaluma has such a wealth of historic buildings that it has the distinction of hosting not just one, but three historic districts. Much of the downtown is listed on the National Register of Historic Places as the Petaluma Historic Commercial District. Within this district are examples of Italianate iron-fronted buildings that are unmatched in all of California. Petaluma also has two local historic districts, the A Street Historic District and the Oakhill Brewster Historic District. Both of these contain broad ranges of vernacular and high style residential designs built from the 1860s through the 1940s. In addition, Petaluma has several individually listed National Register properties, three of which are described in this chapter: the Petaluma Silk Mill, the Carnegie Library and the Post Office.

Along with the chicken ranches and dairies came the need for supporting businesses such as hatcheries, feed stores, creameries and even a chicken pharmacy. Business expansion created new jobs, a demand for housing and increased wealth for Petaluma. Evidence of these prosperous times is reflected in the splendid architecture found throughout Petaluma.

Buildings

associated with transportation come in all shapes and sizes and in some instances have occupied the same property. That is the case with the livery stable that once stood at the corner of D and First Streets.

The McKinney Livery Stable, a Petaluma landmark, represents an early 20th century false-fronted building. Although simple in construction and design, the livery stable is significant for its ability to convey a sense of a bygone era when the horse was the primary form of transportation. Fortunately, when plans to build a parking garage on its site threatened its future, the City required that the livery stable be moved rather than demolished. Today, this piece of Petaluma's history can be found just a few blocks away at the new Steamer Landing Park, where it awaits conversion to an agriculture and river history museum.

Just who McKinney was remains a bit of a mystery. Despite having this name printed on the front of the structure, it is John Grimes and, later, Dr. John E. Tierney with whom many associate

this building. John Grimes, an Englishman, built the structure around 1907. Mr. Grimes boarded and sold horses from this location until 1920, when he sold the property to George P. McNear. McNear leased the building to a veterinarian named John E. Tierney, whom many Petalumans still remember.

Originally from Contra Costa County, Dr. Tierney trained in San Francisco and then set up his practice in Petaluma during the teens. He operated his business out of the livery stable until his death in 1945. Following the death of Dr. Tierney, the building ceased being used for any animal-related purpose, but continued to serve as a reminder of a time when livery stables were an integral part of a successful downtown.

MOVING THE LIVERY STABLE TO STEAMER LANDING PARK

LIVERY STABLE IN STEAMER LANDING PARK

TERRY SMITH

Petaluma's first depot was constructed in 1871 for Colonel Peter Donahue's *San Francisco and North Pacific Railroad*, which later became the *Northwestern Pacific Railroad*. In 1914, the original depot was moved back (southwest) on the railroad property and converted to a freight depot. In its place, a new passenger depot and baggage department were built.

© PETALUMA MUSEUM ASSOCIATION

PETALUMA DEPOT JUST AFTER CONSTRUCTION WAS FINISHED

PHOTO BY KATHERINE J. RINEHART

2005 RENOVATION

COURTESY SONOMA COUNTY LIBRARY

D.J. Patterson, an in-house architect for the *Southern Pacific Railroad*, designed the Mission Revival-style Petaluma Depot in 1913 and local contractor H.P. Vogensen built it. Local subcontractors provided all the labor with the exception of the tile work, which was performed by Cement Tile Manufacturing of San Francisco. Other subcontractors included J.H. Andrews, sheet metal; L.W. Greenwood, plastering; W.S. Harris, plumbing; Thomas and Bauer, electrical work; David Gutermute, painting; Schluckebier Hardware Company, hardware; and Van Bebber Brothers, iron work. Camm and Hedges provided lumber and mill work.

The newly constructed depot and park of the *Northwestern Pacific Railway* was dedicated on April 24, 1914. The completion of the depot came just months before tracks uniting Petaluma and Eureka were laid.

By 1923, at the height of passenger service, the Redwood Empire had become a popular vacation destination, with travelers boarding as far south as Sausalito for a trip to the five North Bay counties.

The Petaluma depot buildings are just a few surviving examples of the Mission Revival architectural style to be found in Petaluma. Even though the depot's importance as a center of transportation declined rapidly in the 1930s with the growing popularity of automobiles and freight trucks, the buildings remain as important symbols of local history and identity. They serve as visual reminders of a past when the train was key to geographic and economic expansion of the region. The City of Petaluma recognized this significance by choosing to rehabilitate the buildings on the depot property. The rehabilitation was completed in 2005 at an estimated cost of $4 million.

Currently the Petaluma Visitors Program occupies the main depot building. The Petaluma Arts Council hopes to locate an arts center in the Railway Express Building in the not too distant future. The Petaluma Rose and Garden Club maintains the 150-plus rose bushes located on the depot grounds.

Petaluma Silk Mill

Looking as if it had been transported from a mill town in New England, this remnant from Petaluma's industrial past is remarkably intact and is therefore historically significant, not only for the city, but for the entire West Coast. In fact, the Petaluma Area Chamber of Commerce labeled Petaluma the "Lowell (Massachusetts) of the West" in 1906. The Silk Mill's stately presence on its large irregular lot illustrates how site considerations — such as proximity to the railroad tracks and the river — were important for these types of buildings. The Silk Mill is located at 450 Jefferson Street, on the edge of a residential neighborhood of 19th and early 20th century worker cottages known today as Old East Petaluma. At one time, there were other factories nearby such as the Nolan-Earle Shoe Company and the Adams Box Factory across Wilson Street.

Designed by a prominent San Francisco architect, Charles I. Havens, this handsome brick textile mill was constructed for the Carlson-Currier Company Silk Manufacturers in 1892. In 1940, Sunset Line and Twine Company bought the building and machinery, beginning production of their fishing lines and specialty cordage. The sound of whirling machines could be heard through the open windows until 2006, when the business finally closed. Over the years, the interior remained remarkably intact — including well-worn floors, metal-clad doors, interior columns, winding tower stairways, and an early fire sprinkler system.

Originally built with one central stair tower, the building was expanded in 1906 and later in 1922. The first addition in 1906 was a silk vault to protect the valuable product. On the day before the 1906 earthquake, a huge fire destroyed nearby buildings and nearly destroyed much finished silk as well.

A 1922 expansion doubled the size of the mill. Brainerd Jones designed the two seamless additions which extend the building to both the north and south. He also added a second tower while retaining the original proportions and overall design. Although the entrance elevation facing the small park along Erwin Street is striking with its regular pattern of multi-pane windows and prominent stair towers, the building's industrial past is well

represented by the utilitarian structures and portions of the building visible along Wilson Street. These features include the tall brick smokestack, a metal frame that once supported a water tower, and several one-story extensions such as the corrugated metal powerhouse for the boiler and a dye house. A heritage palm tree contributes to this landscape, illustrating the age of the complex and complementing its architectural elements. With its listing on the National Register of Historic Places, the mill remains one of the most historically significant buildings illustrating the area's rich industrial past.

MARIA BALES

DAIRYMEN'S FEED ELEVATOR BUILDING

It is hard to pass through Petaluma without taking note of the grain elevators associated with Hunt & Behrens Feed Mill and Dairymen's Feed. Both are located adjacent to the Petaluma River, with Hunt & Behrens at Lakeville Street and Dairymen's Feed on Copeland Street.

The history of Hunt & Behrens dates back to 1921, when Carl N. Behrens and Marvin Hunt established their feed and grain business at the foot of C Street on the Petaluma River so that products could be shipped to and from market by barge.

The two men had experience working at George P. McNear's mill and were inspired by the changes they saw taking place in the animal feed industry — especially the use of vitamins, minerals and proteins as part of animal nutrition. Hunt and Behrens recognized the need for better feeding rations and improved feeding programs. The two men dedicated their operation to two primary goals: customer service and efficiency in production to keep costs low. By keeping to these goals, Hunt & Behrens kept pace with the innovative changes that occurred during the '20s and '30s.

In 1947, Hunt & Behrens moved to its present facility on Lakeville Street, where it initiated the first bulk delivery of mixed feeds. During the 1950s, both the storage and milling facilities were doubled in size. By the 1970s, a second mill had been constructed. The purpose of this second mill was to allow Hunt & Behrens to conduct all its operations under one roof while maintaining the flexibility of operating the poultry feed division separately from the dairy feed division.

Meanwhile, the Poultry Producers of Central California (PPCC) had expanded their feed operation at Copeland and East Washington Streets by building a grain elevator and associated structures in 1938. It could be seen towering "majestically to a height of 170 feet to change the skyline view of the eastside of Petaluma and eclipsing all other buildings in Sonoma County for height" according to one reporter. The Poultry Producers of Central California spent $500,000 on the building and it boasted a storage capacity of 25,000 tons. Included in the price was the cost of the latest in milling machinery. Like Hunt & Behrens, this plant was strategically located next to

COURTESY SONOMA COUNTY LIBRARY

1938 CONSTRUCTION OF
DAIRYMEN'S FEED

HUNT & BEHRENS

the river, allowing shipments of corn and other ingredients to come directly into the mill. Feed was shipped out by train, using spur tracks for the *Northwestern Pacific* and the *Petaluma and Santa Rosa Railroads*.

The PPCC, a large poultry cooperative with more than 6,000 members, went bankrupt in 1964. Many local farmers and ranchers lost the life savings they had invested in the co-op. The plant sat vacant until 1982, when Dairymen's Feed, another cooperative, began using the facility for storage. In 1989, Dairymen's moved their entire operation from 256 Petaluma Boulevard North to the old Poultry Producers facility.

Dave Soren established Dairymen's Feed & Supply Cooperative in 1959. Mr. Soren was a veteran feed man who for many years operated D. Soren & Grain.

Sunrise Farms, a Petaluma-based poultry producer, joined the cooperative in 2007. In addition to dairy feed, Dairymen's now manufactures poultry feed and is expanding their operations to meet the increased business.

Today, both Hunt & Behrens and Dairymen's rely on trucks to transport products to and from their plants. Use of the Petaluma River as a transportation route was eliminated when the drawbridge at Washington Street was replaced with a fixed bridge in 1968. However, there are plans for train service to be restored soon.

COURTESY NORRIS (BOB) DYER

In a town famous

for its poultry production, the Must Hatch Incubator Company at 401 Seventh Street was the largest hatchery operation in the world in 1929. Reflecting this prominence, the building exhibits a sophisticated Mediterranean Renaissance Revival style in the front office pavilion that diagonally faces the street intersection.

The Must Hatch Incubator Company was founded in 1898 by Alphonse E. Bourke, who fabricated artificial incubators of his own design. Several years later, Bourke built a plant on what would become a four-acre site on Seventh Street. This early complex included an incubator factory, a hatchery, and a brooding plant with Leghorn hens. Leo A. Bourke took over the business from his father and expanded it after World War I. In 1923, a devastating fire destroyed the entire complex, including all 612 electric incubators. Leo Bourke immediately rebuilt, but he decided to concentrate entirely on hatchery operations, expanding eventually to a capacity of two million chicks at a single setting. During its heyday, the operation was equipped with 3,890 electric incubators and employed more than 500 people.

The Must Hatch complex once occupied the entire block along Seventh Street with two large hatchery buildings to the south of the office. The 1923 hatchery building no longer stands, but its twin that was added in 1926 remains — its brick façade topped with a Mission revival-shaped parapet. The front portion was used for shipping, while the rear, constructed of hollow clay tile, accommodated the hatchery.

Brainerd Jones designed the 1926 office building. The formal entrance features a two-story tower topped with a Mission tile roof. A row of tall arched windows is set over a shallow portico with a paneled wood door. Along with the intricate and refined brickwork, there is a

delicate floral relief on the concrete pilasters that frame the doorway. Incised above the doorway is the name of the company, preserved despite the building's more recent uses. Must Hatch Incubator Company sold its hatchery in 1958, but it continued operation with new owners until 1989, when this last surviving hatchery in Petaluma ceased operation and the era ended in which Petaluma had reigned supreme in the poultry business.

NORRIS (BOB) DYER

Located at Fourth

and D Streets, Petaluma's attractive Spanish Colonial Revival downtown post office presents a handsome façade. With five tall arched openings and two slightly recessed side pavilions, the symmetrical and compact design illustrates a relatively economical approach for Depression-era public buildings.

This post office is typical of 1930s-era federal buildings erected at a time when art deco ornamentation became popular. Petaluma's post office is notable for its variety of decorative work, including inverted chevrons on the keystones in the arches and a variety of geometric and floral terra cotta trim around the openings and along the frieze. Placed high above the front door at the roofline is an imposing art deco eagle, our national symbol.

John A. McNear's elegant house formerly sat on this lot. Built in the Italianate style in the late 1860s, the house was cleared prior to construction of the post office. McNear's property extended to Fifth Street and included a large garden of exotic trees surrounded by a basalt and lava rock fence. John A. McNear was one of the town's founders, arriving in Petaluma in 1856. He took advantage of the town's early commercial and industrial growth and became a wealthy man.

Newspaper accounts detailed the documents and memorabilia included in the laying of the cornerstone on October 1, 1932. A parade, band music, and other festivities accompanied the formal

ceremony that included the town's officials. The *Petaluma Argus-Courier* noted that "Moving pictures will be taken during the laying of the cornerstone." Funded by the 1926 Keyes-Elliot Act, James Wetmore was the supervising architect for the United States Department of the Treasury out of Washington D.C. Louis A. Simon was the designer. William Spivok of San Francisco was the local contractor.

The understated design of the building features buff textured stucco, mission tiles on the roof, terra cotta trim, and fan-shaped metal window grilles. An intricate decorative metal grille lines the front arches and a dark green classical marble surround frames the front door. Particularly delightful is the addition of six whimsical gargoyle spouts between the arched openings. The interior public lobby has been remodeled slightly over the years, but retains its dark marble floor and wainscoting, its pendant light fixtures, and its original oak paneling.

© PETALUMA MUSEUM ASSOCIATION

SCOTT HESS

ST. JOHN'S CHURCH
JUST AFTER ITS
CONSTRUCTION

Dedicated in 1891, Saint John's Church is a delightful village parish church designed by the eminent English-born architect Ernest Coxhead. Coxhead's California career began in Los Angeles, where he designed 24 churches, 11 of which are still standing. Petaluma is fortunate to have the most historically intact example of a Coxhead church remaining in the state.

The exterior illustrates his inventive incorporation of Renaissance and Medieval design elements into the rustic California Shingle style. The entrance door surround uses tiny Ionic columns supporting oversized classical blocks that in turn support a scrolled pediment. This is a most unusual and visually inventive combination. Tying the exterior composition together, wood shingles cover the low-lying roof and wrap tightly around the curved edges of the surface, then flare out to meet the rough sandstone base.

The interior of Saint John's also features a skilled juxtaposition of contrasting design elements. Upon entering the church from the dim light of the tower room, one notices the lofty spatial quality of the open timberwork ceiling in the nave. The side arcade is surprisingly low and rests on a short column, but there is the feeling of one large assembly space when seated. Dark woodwork creates a warm interior that continues the design elements seen on the exterior — such as the Ionic columns and the ribbon and garland carved relief designs. One of the most impressive Arts and Crafts details is the exposed double-dovetail joinery in the oak pews, wainscoting, and side doors.

In 1856, Saint John's Episcopal Church was established in Petaluma. Four years later in 1860, the parish constructed a simple pioneer church on the corner lot Isaac Wickersham had purchased for $200. In 1890, the building was moved further down along C Street to make room for the construction of the present-day church. Local firms completed the job, notably Camm and Sims as contractor and Evan Brothers as masons. The parish also decided to specify an expensive concrete foundation under the stone instead of the more typical brick.

Today, the church complex includes the 1950 church offices and classrooms next door and a 1956 parish hall that replaced the original pioneer building when it burned in 1947. Often showcased as one of Coxhead's most successful Shingle style designs, Saint John's sits solidly and comfortably within the A Street Historic Residential District at Fifth and C Streets.

ST. VINCENT DE PAUL CHURCH

The 100-foot towers of this impressive Romanesque Revival church dominate not only the tiny triangular Liberty Park but also the townscape near and far. Restored and refurbished in 1994, its beautiful exterior and interior are stylistic links to ecclesiastical designs of earlier centuries.

On January 18, 1857, Saint Vincent de Paul became the second Roman Catholic parish in Sonoma County. By this time, several other denominations in Petaluma — such as the Episcopal and Methodist communities — had formed local churches in the growing settlement. Located originally on the southeast corner of Keokuk and Prospect Streets, this pioneer church served both for services and a school. In 1876, the parish built a wood frame Gothic Revival church on newly acquired property bounded by Western, Bassett, Liberty and Howard Streets.

In 1926, the parish sold its 1876 Gothic-Revival building to Elim Lutheran Church, and it was moved to Baker and Stanley Streets. This cleared the site for the edifice that today is a Petaluma landmark. Before construction began on April 24, 1926, the San Francisco architect Leo J. Devlin presented an artistic rendering that emphasized the building's height and commanding presence in the neighborhood. It would be an amazing structure for a small river town. Even though the exterior is traditional Romanesque Revival design, the construction incorporates a modern steel skeleton and reinforced concrete. Leibert and Trobock were the contractors. Two years after groundbreaking, on May 26, 1928, the $200,000 church was dedicated with much fanfare.

COURTESY PETALUMA VISITORS PROGRAM

Among the notable features that draw inspiration from the medieval Romanesque are the two ornate bell towers at the corners, the three arched entrance doors, the large rose windows, and the clay tile roof. The domed tower roof is inlaid with multi-color clay tiles — surprisingly accented with tiles representing each of the California missions. The narrow vestibule with its clay-tiled floor leads into the spacious main body of the church, a tall barrel-vaulted central space with an arcade separating the side aisles. The capitals of the columns supporting the arcade consist of swirls of leaves and incised intertwining patterns inspired by Moorish design.

The elaborate main altar of Italian marble sits within a large semi-circular apse. Hanging toward the right of the altar is a sanctuary lamp that came from the previous church building. The bell in the southeast tower came from the original church as well. Oak pews, marbleized plaster, and a large number of stained glass windows crafted in Munich, Germany, complete the richly finished interior.

The church property also includes a rectory and a church hall, both completed in 1916. The most recent building project was the creation of a plaza in 2001. Bassett Street in front of the church was closed to traffic and paved. The church steps were extended, and a fountain was installed. This project extends the park to the church, provides space for the church community to gather, and enhances the entire neighborhood.

SCOTT HESS

LUIS PADILLA

CARNEGIE LIBRARY
CONSTRUCTION NEARS
COMPLETION

© PETALUMA MUSEUM ASSOCIATION

JOANN NAYLOR

What we know today

as the Petaluma Historical Library and Museum at 20 Fourth Street was originally a Carnegie Free Library. Petaluma was one of the earliest communities to apply for and receive Carnegie funding. The first request for funds, made by the Ladies Improvement Club in 1896, met with no response. A second request made by the Library Trustees, many of whom were married to members of the Ladies Improvement Club, was submitted in 1900.

In January, 1901, a $12,500 grant was awarded to the City. It included the usual Carnegie stipulation that the City provide the land and pass a tax that would generate annually an amount equal to 10% of the grant for the support and maintenance of the building. Petaluma met the challenge, thanks largely to Addie Attwater, President of the Ladies Improvement Club. She sold the land upon which the library would be built to the City of Petaluma at a reduced rate, stipulating that the land and any improvements would revert to her or her heirs should the building no longer serve as a library.

Brainerd Jones, a promising young Petaluma architect, was selected to design a splendid building that exemplifies the City's civic achievements. Jones' design for the building reflects the influence of the classically inspired Chicago World's Fair and the rise of the City Beautiful movement.

Craftsmen responsible for the construction of the library were local and included Richard W. Moller as general contractor; James R. Nesbitt, who constructed the massive concrete foundations which extend to bedrock; William C. Stradling, who did the brick and stone work; and E.W.M. Evans, a stone mason who donated California granite for the cornerstone and is responsible for the four entrance columns.

The interior is one large room, filled with light from all directions through the first and second floor windows and skylight. Four tapered fluted columns establish a central square, open to the surrounding second floor gallery and to the vaulted ceiling with its leaded glass sunburst dome. The dome is believed to be the largest free-standing stained glass dome in California. The central floral design is red and gold, with intricate geometric patterns radiating outward in shades of blue and gold with red. The rim of the dome is encircled in lights.

Douglas fir facing of the columns, and of the beams they support, conceals the building's structural components. Throughout the interior, Douglas fir is used in the framing of the windows and the skylight, in the wainscoting, in the gallery rail, and for the well-crafted turned spindles that surround the open central space. Douglas fir was also used for the double staircase that rises from either side of the front entrance to the gallery. At the landing, the wainscot provides a graceful curve from the three round portico windows to the arched windows on either side with their wood-framed sunburst pattern. The fir is treated with a clear finish through which the grain is revealed, even though the finish has darkened with age. Off-white plaster walls and ceiling contrast with the dark paneling and help create the even distribution of light throughout the interior.

The exterior of this wood framed building is faced with locally quarried "sandstone" and Alameda pressed brick. Stone was transported from the Stony Point Quarry located about nine miles northwest of town by way of the electric Petaluma and Santa Rosa Railway, which coincidentally owned the quarry. The stone is described in *Structural and Industrial Materials of California* as a trachytic lava that resembles San Jose sandstone so much that the people of Sonoma County often erroneously call it "sandstone."

The cornerstone was laid June 4, 1904, with much civic celebration. The library opened its doors on February 17, 1906, for a festive public viewing prior to its completion and transfer of books from the previous library on the third floor of City Hall. The official opening was not until November 13, 1906, due to some damage that occurred during the April 18, 1906 earthquake.

With very little change, the building served as a library until 1976, when a new library was constructed. The Carnegie building was then rehabilitated for use as a historical library and museum. The building was listed on the National Register of Historic Places in 1988.

KAREN PHILLIPS

Schools can be major

identifying characteristics of a town and integral parts of its neighborhoods. Lincoln Primary and the Philip Sweed School are such buildings. Both were designed using classical proportions, with a central bay and entrance with columns and shallow porticos. The classrooms flank each side symmetrically, with grouped windows indicating the individual classrooms. Unfortunately, neither school is being used any longer for its intended purpose. Through adaptive reuse, however, they are both still major architectural contributors to the residential landscape.

© PETALUMA MUSEUM ASSOCIATION

LINCOLN PRIMARY SCHOOL

The Lincoln Primary School was designed by Brainerd Jones in 1911 in a neoclassical style to replace the B Street School that had been located on this site. The school was constructed in record time. On December 13, 1910, the Board of Education let the contract for the construction of the building to J.O. Kuykendall of San Francisco. The building was to be completed by July 15, 1911, but the contractor actually finished the work more than a month ahead of schedule and the dedication ceremony was held on August 4, 1911. Part of the dedication included a presentation by a special guest, Charles Kubie — a Petaluma resident since 1857 — who had been present at the laying of the cornerstone for the B Street School in 1859.

At the time of its construction, the Lincoln Primary School was the only school in Petaluma to have its own auditorium. It boasted a seating capacity of about three hundred.

In later years, the Petaluma City School administrative offices were located in the building. Those offices were relocated in 1997 and the building was sold to an Emeryville developer who converted the school for commercial use.

The school is a significant contributor to the A Street Historic District, which became Petaluma's first locally designated historic district in 1986.

STAFF AND STUDENTS OF SWEED SCHOOL — STAFF UPPER RIGHT, RIGHT TO LEFT: ANNE HOPKINS, HERMINA FREYSCHLAG, MABEL PUTNAM, INEZ MACDONALD, ALICE STAUFFER

SWEED SCHOOL

Local architect Brainerd Jones designed the Philip Sweed School at 331 Keller Street in 1927. The new elementary school was built on the site of the Hill High School building. Thomas B. Goodwin of San Francisco was the general contractor. Years earlier, Goodwin had worked on the Petaluma High School and Petaluma Junior High School projects, both located on Fair Street.

The school was named in honor of Philip Sweed, a prominent Petaluma educator who served as president of the Petaluma Board of Education for more than three decades. He was also a successful merchant. Mr. Sweed did not live to see the school built. He died from influenza just weeks after the contract for the school was awarded.

The $75,000 elementary school was dedicated on January 15, 1928, with a grand ceremony involving the Native Sons and Native Daughters of the Golden West. Sweed School opened on January 23, 1928. Mabel Putnam served as its first principal, alongside teachers Anne Hopkins, Inez McDonald, Alice Stauffer and Hermina Freyschlag.

Like the Lincoln Primary School, the Philip Sweed School is in a local historic district — the Oakhill Brewster Historic District. Guidelines are in place which assured that, when the school was recently rehabilitated for use as condominiums, the work met design and material criteria respectful of the existing historic and architectural character of the neighborhood.

LEFT TO RIGHT: ENGINEER/PARAMEDIC STEVE CURTIS, FIREFIGHTER CRAIG MARSTON, CAPTAIN CHUCK GOUCHER AND FIREFIGHTER/PARAMEDIC BLAKE MCGREW WITH PETALUMA FIRE DEPARTMENT'S NEWEST AND OLDEST FIRE ENGINES

FIRE DEPARTMENT

The Petaluma Fire Station on D Street represents one of the few Art Deco buildings in Petaluma. The station was built on a vacant lot in 1938 for $45,000 — of which $18,180 was funded by a Public Works Administration grant. George P. McNear donated the land upon which the fire station sits to the City of Petaluma in 1926. Petaluma architect Brainerd Jones prepared the plans and specifications, and Adam Arras & Sons of San Francisco were the building contractors.

Hundreds gathered at the Fire Station on July 23, 1938, to witness the dedication of what was considered at the time to be one of the most modern stations in the United States.

The façade of the Fire Station is arranged in a series of setbacks that is characteristic of the Art Deco style. Also in keeping with Art Deco style are the angular composition and vertical emphasis. These elements were respected as part of the 1970 Second Street addition that was designed by Dick Lieb. The fire department is currently planning to construct a new facility on Petaluma Boulevard South between E and F Streets.

Herold Building

Originally the site of the Washington Stable and Livery, this two-story commercial brick building was constructed by local contractor Samuel Rodd for Angela Canepa, an enterprising widow who invested extensively in Petaluma property in 1899.

The two bay windows facing Kentucky Street differ slightly. One is curved and one is angled. The building was extended to include two additional bays in 1923. Notable features on the first floor are iron columns, ornamental detail work, and large transom windows with prism glass. Capitalizing on the corner lot, the central architectural feature that crowns the bay windowed second floor is the corner tower with curved windows and metal conical roof. The bell-shaped cap was removed in the 1960s, but reconstructed in 1987.

Herold Drug Store occupied the corner of the first floor for many years and their name remains on the inlay sign on the threshold. The upper floor offices have continuously served various small businesses and professionals since the building was constructed. Retaining much of the original design and materials, there is a wide hallway with original wood trim, a central skylight, and vintage restrooms.

SCOTT HESS

Scattered throughout

the historic downtown are good examples of buildings constructed of brick and iron cladding with decorative features. These date from the 1870s and 1880s when this type of construction became popular. Not only was this manner of building thought to make these buildings fireproof, but it was considered a way to create fashionable buildings with elaborate designs mass produced economically in a foundry. Some of the best examples of iron front buildings are located in a continuous row on the south side of Western Avenue between Petaluma Boulevard (once Main Street) and Kentucky Street.

SCOTT HESS

MASONIC BUILDING

The Masonic Building, at 49 Petaluma Boulevard North, was built in 1882 on the site of the old Union Hotel. This corner Italianate with a prominent clock tower features arched windows at each floor and a bracketed eave. Like the other buildings on this block, the exterior is a combination of cast iron over brick. John McNear sold the lot to the Masons for $6,750. The cornerstone was laid on September 9, 1881, with a celebration that included a special train, speeches, and a Grand Ball.

The street level accommodated retail stores and offices. The upper floors have always been reserved for the Masonic organization. The Seth Thomas clock was manufactured in Connecticut and came up the river on a steamer. Its original wood housing was replaced in 1934 when a copper-clad tower roof was built. In 1994, an elevator was installed during a renovation of the building.

The Mutual Relief Building, at 19 Western Avenue, is the crowning glory of the block of iron front buildings. It was built in 1885 for the Mutual Relief Society, a community life insurance organization. Italian Renaissance detailing is found in the rich decoration and elaborate window surrounds — all in cast iron. Behind the iron is smooth stuccoed brick. What further distinguishes this building is the developed central bay with complex layers of ornamentation, including columns painted in faux marble. Recently painted and updated, the building was the recipient of a federal tax credit for historic preservation projects.

At one time Dr. E. S. Lippitt, a local professor and lawyer, had his office on the second floor. He is reputed to have had the largest law library in Northern California. Today the rooms have been converted into rental units, complete with exceptionally tall ceilings and views of the downtown area. Over the years, the top floor was used as a ballroom and lodge hall. Later it functioned as a rehearsal room for Petaluma's town band. An historic "Coca-Cola" sign is painted on the brick back wall. Through the efforts of Heritage Homes of Petaluma, the sign has been repainted to preserve the delightful hatchling that represented Petaluma's claim to fame.

Other notable iron front buildings in downtown include the Odd Fellows Hall at 107 Petaluma Boulevard, built in 1877, and the former Petaluma Opera House at 145 Kentucky Street. The 1886 McNear Building and the Fritsch & Zartman Building are also outstanding examples of iron front construction.

ASHLEY WILSON

© PETALUMA MUSEUM ASSOCIATION

MUTUAL RELIEF BUILDING, 2007 BUTTER & EGG DAYS PARADE

TERRY SMITH

FIRST MCNEAR BUILDING, CIRCA 1908

MCNEAR BUILDINGS

John A. McNear, Sr., was a founder of Petaluma. He came to town in 1856 with his wife Clara. Clara's father, George Williams, was already living in Petaluma and had established the Washington Hotel. Not long after settling in Petaluma, John McNear became a major figure in the development of the city. He built his grain and shipping business into a major concern and was involved in numerous real estate ventures. He was responsible for building many downtown structures, including the High Victorian Italianate building constructed in 1886, shown above. The building fills a trapezoidal lot with no two sides parallel. Both the Fourth Street and Petaluma Boulevard sides of the building possess cast iron façades. Each façade has a classical entablature with narrow, closely spaced, arched windows below. Pilasters add to the vertical appearance. Other details are sculptured heads, flowers and filigree cresting. Lettering on the delicate castings states their manufacturer: "O'Connell & Lewis Architectural Iron Work, 230-236 Steuart Street, San Francisco". Note the partial stone wall visible from the Fourth Street side of the building. Research suggests that the stone was specifically used as a construction

material and is not a remnant of an earlier building that stood on what is now a vacant lot between the LanMart and McNear buildings.

In 1911 John A. McNear, Sr., hired Brainerd Jones to design a building that would adjoin his existing building. W.R. Haskins and William Stradling were the contractors.

This two-story building was planned to conform to the irregular lot it sits upon. It also has two frontages — on Petaluma Boulevard and on Fourth Street. When it was built, the first floor consisted of a theater and three stores. The upper floor was designed to accommodate office suites and lodge rooms that included a kitchen, dining room and other amenities.

At the time of its construction, the McNear Building covered more ground than any other business building in the city. In order to build the structures, several shanties associated with the Chinese community were demolished.

The Mystic Theater was the inspiration of Dr. John A. McNear, Jr., and was originally designed as a vaudeville house and motion picture theatre. The theatre opened to the public on January 25, 1912, and was managed by Dr. McNear for many years.

By the 1970s, the building in general was in poor repair, as was its neighbor, the other McNear building. Fortunately for Petaluma, Jeff Harriman and Wally Lourdeaux purchased the buildings and spent $500,000 to restore these landmarks. Their efforts inspired a downtown revitalization from which we continue to benefit today.

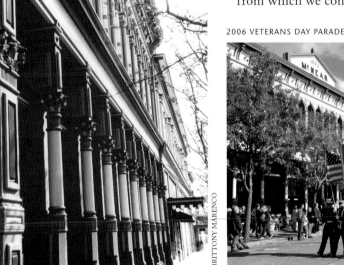

2006 VETERANS DAY PARADE

At the time of its construction, the McNear Building covered more ground than any other business building in the city. In order to build the structures, several shanties associated with the Chinese community were demolished.

The beautifully restored iron front at 119 Petaluma Boulevard North was constructed sometime between 1883 and 1885 and was first associated with William Zartman and John Fritsch, manufacturers of buggies and wagons. They established their blacksmith forge on the site in 1852. Fritsch and Zartman appear to have incorporated portions of earlier brick and stone one-story structures into the stately two-story Italianate building we see today.

In 1893, Ira B. Raymond arrived in Petaluma and opened a notions store. The following year his brother Henry J. Raymond joined him in the enterprise. In 1896 they moved their business — which became known as the Racket Store — into the Fritsch and Zartman building. The business thrived and the brothers eventually purchased the building and changed the name of their store to Raymond Brothers. By 1917, Raymond Brothers was a full-fledged department store, offering furniture, bedding, carpets, window shades and more.

By 1930 the Raymond Brothers had moved to Kentucky Street, and the Leader opened at 119 Petaluma Boulevard North. Leader was replaced by J.C. Penney in 1941. Harry Empey was managing the store in 1952 when the building was completely remodeled and the stucco "slip cover" was placed over the original plaster-over-brick façade. At the time, Josephine Gwinn, widow of prominent Petaluma banker, Harry Gwinn, owned the building. The property has been in the Gwinn family since the 1920s.

Stephen Lind, Mrs. Gwinn's grandson and a fourth generation Petaluman, now owns the building. Mr. Lind took advantage of City of Petaluma's Storefront Improvement Loan Program to remove the "slip cover" and bring this building back to its former glory. Others responsible for the transformation include project manager Joe Hutka, architect Mary Dooley, and architectural historian Nancy Stoltz. Skilled craftsmen from Hindz Brothers of Santa Rosa did the restoration work and the painting contractor was Rainbow Painting and Waterproofing of San Francisco.

119 PETALUMA BOULEVARD NORTH IN 1959

COURTESY SONOMA COUNTY LIBRARY

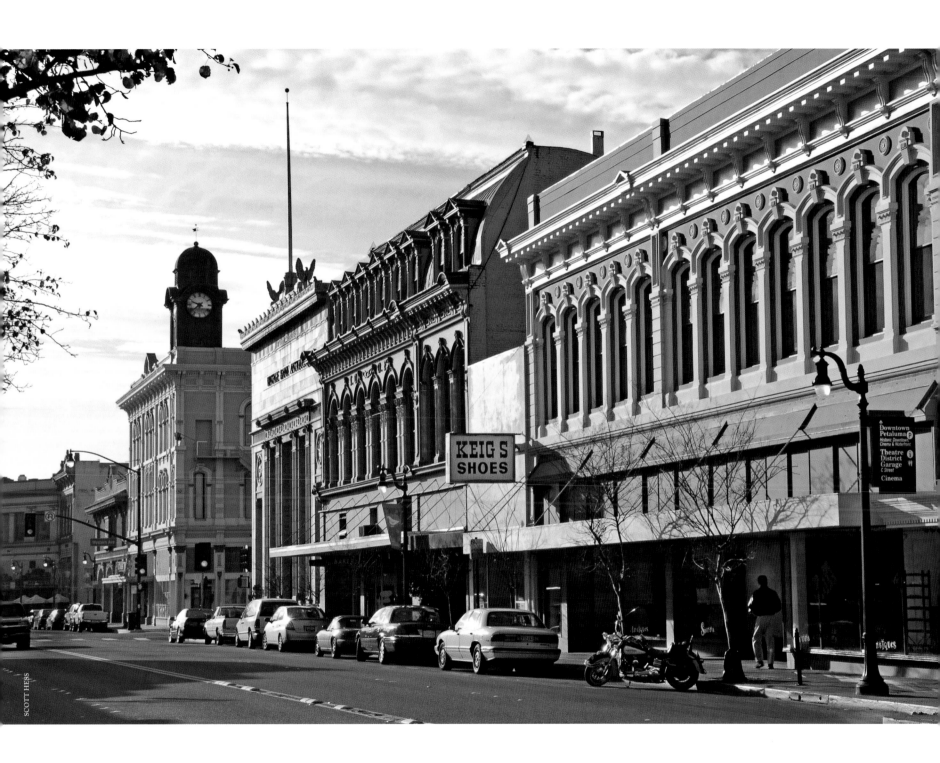

95 Celebrating Petaluma

HOTEL PETALUMA BOOSTERS, 1922

Frederick Whitton, a San Francisco architect, designed this elegant five-story Mediterranean-style building, which was dedicated as the Hotel Petaluma on April 10, 1924. The total cost of the structure and the lot was $325,000, but $250,000 of that total was paid for by subscription as part of a Petaluma Area Chamber of Commerce campaign. A board of directors managed the hotel and held the property in trust for more than 850 stockholders.

The hotel was equipped with Petaluma's first passenger elevator. The building was steam heated throughout, the steam being provided by two oil-burning boilers installed in the basement. The rooms on the fifth floor were reserved for employees, while the second, third and fourth floors consisted of a total of 89 guestrooms, 63 of which had private bathrooms.

The main entrance to the Hotel Petaluma was on Kentucky Street. Guests walked through an elegant open-air courtyard with a water fountain and slate-covered patio. Longtime Petaluma resident John Pedroni remembers when this area was enclosed and converted to the Lanai Room, a popular coffee shop and cocktail lounge that was open during World War II. The décor was Polynesian and it was a trendy spot for the younger crowd and the military men stationed at Two Rock. During this time period, volunteer spotters searched the skies for enemy planes as they sat in a 12 square foot shelter, with windows on all sides, on the hotel roof. They were responsible for reporting all aircraft seen flying over Petaluma by phone to the West Coast Defense Center.

By the 1950s, the Redwood Room had replaced the Lanai as the popular nightspot in the Hotel Petaluma. It was located on the corner of the building where retail shops are currently found.

The Elks Lodge bought the building in 1959, by which time the property had long been used as a residential hotel. The Elks sold the building to the current owners in 1994.

NOTE ROOFTOP BUILDING FOR WWII PLANE SPOTTERS

Two prominent

1920s bank buildings anchor each end of the major commercial block on Petaluma Boulevard between Western Avenue and Washington Street. Both are excellent examples of the classically inspired designs that were typical during that time.

SONOMA COUNTY NATIONAL BANK

The Sonoma County Bank Building at 199 Petaluma Boulevard North was constructed in 1925, as is boldly inscribed along the frieze of the elegantly curved façade. H. H. Winner Company designed this prominently-sited banking temple on a busy corner intersection. Like the American Trust Company, this Roman Renaissance Revival building is clad in terracotta to simulate masonry. Above the frieze is a projecting cornice topped with a classical balustrade. It seems to need a similarly tall building next door to the south, but photographs show the neighbors have always been just one story — even before the clock shop was built.

The curved entry is framed by a tall arch and is notable for its bronze and glass decoration. The double-height interior features pink marble and a decorated plasterwork ceiling with large rosettes and traces of the original gold leaf in place. On the south wall are low relief inset panels, one of which features griffins, or winged lions.

In 1930, this building became the Sonoma County branch of the Bank of America. The Petaluma branch of Bank of America was located across the street on the site of the present Bank of America.

The Sonoma County branch of the Bank of America remained at 199 Petaluma Boulevard North until the 1970s. Since that time, the building has been home to Westgate Realty, Legacy Marketing and most recently Monarch Interiors. Notice the brass compass in the sidewalk in front of the entrance.

1947 PHOTO COURTESY SONOMA COUNTY LIBRARY

JULIA WELCH

The American Trust Company Building at 101 Petaluma Boulevard North was designed in 1926 by Hyman & Appleton Architects of San Francisco. This address was the earlier site of the Whitney Block owned by Albion Whitney, a grocery store proprietor. The American Trust Company Building is an elegant classic bank building clad in terracotta with many decorative details, including open-winged eagles flanking the flagpole. The sailing ship emblems of the former bank are still visible on the exterior. The exterior terracotta simulates unpolished granite. The high foundation is genuine granite, affording a good opportunity to compare the two.

In 1960, American Trust merged with Wells Fargo Bank, which stayed at this location until 1987. In 1995, the building ceased functioning as a bank and was converted into an antique cooperative. The cages and marble finishes were dismantled to make room for its new use.

AMERICAN TRUST COMPANY BUILDING IN 2007

JIM JOHNSON, STUDIO 7

CONCLUSION

The landmarks presented on the preceding pages represent a valuable heritage from earlier generations and illustrate aspects of Petaluma's character that cannot be communicated in any other manner. Neither photographs nor narratives nor dim memories can substitute for the authentic symbols of the past that continue to stand within the city. We are fortunate to have a remarkable collection of commercial, institutional, residential, industrial and agricultural resources that give this community its unique visual identity.

As we plan for the future, the quality of design, materials and craftsmanship exhibited by these buildings should serve as an inspiration to those constructing the landmarks of tomorrow. Meanwhile, the citizens of Petaluma rely on organizations such as the Petaluma Museum Association and Heritage Homes of Petaluma to continue their efforts to preserve and promote Petaluma's historic and architectural legacy.

SEVEN

THE WORLD'S GREATEST EGG BASKET
by Norris (Bob) Dyer

"Petaluma is the boss chicken town of the Pacific Coast. The man who eats genuine fresh eggs — not the cold storage kind — in San Francisco may thank Petaluma hens, for more than half the eggs are from this place."

Petaluma Weekly Budget, 1898

BYCE AND THE MACHINE — THE EARLY DAYS

PREVIOUS PAGE: A SMALL FLOCK OF CHICKENS, TYPICAL OF THE EARLY DAYS
RIGHT PAGE: PETALUMA INCUBATOR COMPANY, CIRCA 1905
BELOW: PETALUMA INCUBATOR

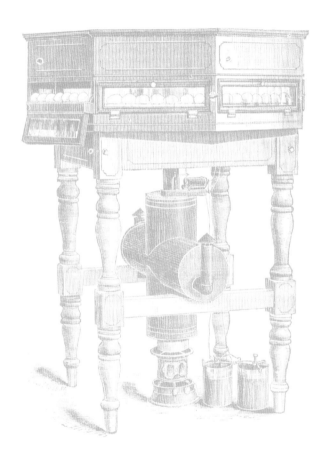

LYMAN BRYCE

In the 1800s most chicken eggs came from small backyard flocks, managed by the farmer's wife. Eggs had long been popular as they could be prepared quickly for the table, and were used frequently for baking. Consequently, demand continued to increase. Both the Egyptians and the Chinese were masters of artificial egg incubation. The latter required workers to crawl into pre-heated ovens from which the fire had been removed, and place the eggs in baskets around the floor of the oven, enduring temperatures of 103 degrees while doing so.

The first mechanical incubators were patented in this country as early as the 1840s, but farmers had to wait decades before the first practical model became available. That challenge was finally met by Petaluman Lyman C. Byce in the 1880s (with the help of several other inventors).

But the real catalyst for the first widely and successfully marketed incubator came about only when he suffered a toothache in the spring of 1879 and visited a local dentist. There he met Dr. Isaac Dias who already had the functioning incubator that would soon be patented.

An 1881 edition of the Pacific Rural Press pictured the original Petaluma incubator. The accompanying article indicated that the machine was the "joint invention of Messrs. T. R. Jacobs and I.L. Dias of Petaluma, and patented through Dewey & Co. Agency." Note there was no mention of Byce at that point. What followed was a long technical description of the device briefly summarized below:

- Octagonal in shape with glass access doors on each side;
- Each of the eight pans can be removed without disturbing the other;
- Stands on three-foot legs which also support the heater;
- Hot air enters oven in the center;
- Has fancy valve and temperature regulator to "perfectly govern the heat";
- Has capacity of 260 eggs; and
- Incubation takes three weeks

Where was Byce when the machine was first sold? Well, we do know he arrived in Petaluma from Canada in 1878 in his late 20s to "find a particular kind of climate that would be suited to my wants, as I came for my health." This is from an interview for a 1930 poultry magazine. Obviously, the town must have suited him as he lived here until 1944, dying at the age of 91! The magazine lionized him for his earlier work as a sort of Petaluman Thomas Edison:

> "Laboring at the task until late at night, early at the task the following morning, scarcely pausing for meals, the flight of time was not noticed by Mr. Byce, so interesting had his work become. After a 20-hour day, the shavings from his work bench were brushed off, blankets were spread thereon, and he indulged in but a few hours of rest and recuperation."

Byce did do a lot of research, verifying, from trials with his chickens, for example, that the optimum temperature for incubation was 103 degrees. He also had good ideas for an incubator heat regulator. But the real catalyst for the first widely and successfully marketed incubator came about only when he suffered a toothache in the spring of 1879 and visited a local dentist, Dr. Isaac Dias. Dias already had a functioning incubator that would soon be patented. Byce and Dias formed the Petaluma Incubator Company in 1882 and worked together on prototypes. Soon afterward in 1884, Dias died in a hunting accident.

Byce then wound up taking over the company, after initially displaying reluctance to "go on with the business." The third inventor, T.R. Jacobs, played no obvious future role in the concern. Byce claimed, to his death, that the Petaluma Incubator was his sole invention.

An interesting and very busy envelope that Petaluma postal expert Donald Scott dates from 1886 shows yet a different, smaller incubator for $20 and a brooder for only $10. Curiously, it does not promote the "Petaluma Incubator Company" but rather, its products, and all of the awards the machines had already garnered.

Historians credit Christopher Nisson and Lyman Byce as individuals responsible for the development of the poultry industry in Petaluma. Nisson showed as early as 1882, with his 2,000 laying hens, that large flocks of chickens could be successfully managed. He created the first hatchery about 1899. This would eventually become Petaluma Hatchery which remained in business until 1958. Byce's machine did the rest. By 1900 Byce had sold more than 20,000 of them. Ads from that year picture a 200-egg version of the incubator. Further acclaim and increased sales resulted when one of his incubators won a Gold Medal at the Louisiana Purchase Exposition in 1904. A hundred other incubators from all over the country crowded the market by 1908, but Byce persevered, using clever marketing, and generating publicity whenever he could. At one fair he demonstrated how his machine could also hatch goose, turkey and even ostrich eggs! His first state-of-the-art production facility was opened on Main Street in 1904, and by that time he already was one of the largest employers in town with around 100 on his company's staff.

Author Thea Lowry, writing in *Empty Shells,* also felt that "His [Byce] inventions laid the golden-egg shaped cornerstone of Petaluma's prosperous poultry kingdom."

A brochure by Conley & Lamb, Real Estate, published in early 1904, already termed Petaluma "the Chicken Center of the World." The City:

> "…ships annually an average of 300 cases per day, or 10,800 dozen eggs. This represents an income of $3,000 per day, or over $1,000,000 per year."

Bank deposits were already $1,600,000 — all this money at a time where the realtor advertised bargains such as the following: "$1000 — Lot 50' x 100'; good house of 6 rooms; small barn; 1 chicken house."

The boom was on.

"With all of Petaluma's sources of prosperity, the latest is the biggest and the most prominent. The poultry industry is now the one that outranks all the rest. It is Chickaluma now…

"Petaluma's output of eggs and poultry for 1905 was 3,827,061 dozen eggs and 39,392 chickens. The favorable location and climate have had much to do with building up Petaluma and her varied industries, but greater than all else is the fact of having a free salt-water highway to San Francisco."

Frank H. Snow, 1906

WHITE LEGHORN CHICKS

ABOVE: INTERIOR, HATCHERY, CIRCA 1910;   BELOW: BROODER

SINGLE COMB WHITE LEGHORN ROOSTER

"The White Leghorn rarely wants to sit; she lays most industriously; she is hardy; she begins to lay when very young."

W. S. Harwood, 1908

Although Lyman Byce

and Christopher Nisson started their businesses using Brown Leghorns, by the turn of the century the predominant chicken in Petaluma flocks was the Single Comb White Leghorn (SCWL). The hen of this variety was not known for producing much meat and was better suited to become a virtual egg factory, because of its nervous temperment and broodiness. Harwood estimates that there were already 1,000,000 hens in the Petaluma area by 1908. At that time, he claimed at least 75 percent of the county's population raised poultry. In rather blunt terms, typical of the era, he stated: "It is not an occupation relegated to grandmothers. It is a man's occupation. It requires sagacity, tact, experience, and knowledge. There are many who fail but they are those who come ill-prepared, lacking in application, inadequate in knowledge — but those who are fit, those who make it their chief business not a side-issue, earn handsome incomes."

To support his premise, he cited the success of one rancher with a flock of about 10,000 hens who was making a net profit of $6,000 a year. Already, chicken houses and brooders were everywhere, as well as large hatcheries.

In 1915, a visitor commented that "the hillsides and valleys are dotted with snowy flocks of fowls, and farmers on the road are either bringing in cases of eggs or taking out sacks of grain."

It was not just the Petaluma chicken farmers getting wealthy from their SCWL's but also collateral enterprises, an example being feed and grain mills. One of them, Coulson's Poultry and Stock Food Company, was a Petaluma mainstay for over forty years. It was founded by A.R. Coulson right after the turn of the century. Coulson started out as a sort of chicken doctor, even producing a lice killer (effective enough to also kill bedbugs), but eventually became known for his special food mixes. As early as 1903 there were advertisements for his "Egg and Feather Food" and "Chick Food." Pictured is a handy little note pad the company gave out. The item is undated and without

COULSON'S POULTRY AND STOCK FOOD COMPANY SOUVENIR NOTEPAD

an address although the company was then located at 250-256 Main Street. It continued in business until the early 1940s.

A Chamber of Commerce brochure from 1916 stated that the total production of eggs in 1915 had increased to 14,601,417 dozen. The Chamber's brochure was a clarion call to join the chicken industry in Petaluma where eggs were now getting as much as 52¢ a dozen — more than double what they were going for a decade earlier — and fryers were going for $4.50 per dozen. The brochure suggested a "nest-egg" (excuse the expression) of some $3,000 to purchase five acres of land, a modest house, wagon, tools, and 1,000 pullets, leaving an estimated $450 until the first eggs were ready for market.

Charles Weeks, in *Egg Farming in California* (circa 1918), echoed the Chamber's call and sang of the blessings of a rural life:

> "To the man who loves animal and plant life, who revels in the sunshine out under the open sky, who is intoxicated with the fresh air and vigor of an outside life, to this man the poultry business is an ideal business. To the man who loves close rooms and musty volumes there is little for him in the poultry business. But if you love freedom, love independence, and like to be your own master, then go out on a poultry ranch and live the natural life."

There would be more of this kind of communication after Bert Kerrigan arrived in Petaluma.

BERT KERRIGAN REIGNS — 1918-1927

"Truly God has been good to this community with its crystal mountain water, clear sunshine and tempered breezes. The very earth seems to radiate with all the blessings of nature, and from it all comes the health, contentment and prosperity that has made this city famous as the egg center of the world, and one of the more productive dairying and diversified farming sections in California.

"Petaluma has proved that the lowly hen egg is without peer in food value. It is nature's health builder for eating and cooking, and can't be substituted. For invalids and children and for the man who works, it has been and will be almost indispensable. And eggs contain more nutriment per ounce for less money compared to other foods.

"Petaluma is the richest city according to the number of its population (6,000) of any city in the United States."

Herbert (Bert) Kerrigan, 1921

Although egg production was up, the price fell to 47¢ a dozen by 1918 and other industries were being hit hard by WW I economic woes. Even Lyman Byce and the Petaluma Incubator Company were not spared. The 40-year-old company failed due to a growing inventory and flagging payments from overseas. He declared bankruptcy in 1919. Eventually, the firm would re-emerge as the Petaluma Electric Incubator Company under his younger son, Wilbert Elwood Byce. Things would never be as good for the new company because of heavy competition from such firms as the Petersime Electric Company of Ohio. There is even a photograph showing several large truckloads of the Petersime electric incubators being delivered to Petaluma!

In 1918 the Chamber of Commerce reached out and found Herbert Kerrigan. For about a decade, from 1918-1928, he would be cock-of-the-walk in Petaluma — a full-steam-ahead, smooth-talking and smooth-writing update of P.T. Barnum. Instead of circuses, it would be parades featuring giant chickens and eggs, beauty queens, and National Egg Day. Kerrigan had helped San Francisco recover after the earthquake. Following a local survey of our chicken assets, he came up with some snappy P.R. slogans for the city. The Chamber liked "The World's Egg Basket" and within a few years, most of the country's egg-lovers would know us by this handle, or a variant, "Egg Basket of the World". Soon the name was in wide use.

Bert Kerrigan's concept of a National Egg Day first required a whirlwind campaign to get Washington's buy-in. It was followed by a cascade of pamphlets and news releases, and finally, the first big annual parade down Main Street with an Egg Queen on August 31, 1918. The Chamber President, Harry W. Gwinn, inspired the construction of a giant egg basket, 15 feet long, 10 feet high and 5 feet wide. All this was enough to garner national publicity and Hollywood cameras. An illustration shows Kerrigan standing immediately to the left of the basket with its slogan and 1918 egg statistics. There were 4,000,000 Petaluma hens, laying 37,500,000 dozen eggs annually. Kerrigan expounded:

> "Our great objective will be to educate the people of the food value in the lowly egg. Every float, every special unit, every window in Petaluma, every district participating, must keep this in mind and tell it so well the world will see and appreciate."

The yearly election of Egg Queen was an egalitarian event with nominees listed in the *Petaluma Argus-Courier* and the winner announced after a popular vote. In 1921, the winner was Marjorie Park. She got to ride astride her egg chariot. Her crown had been presented by California Governor William D. Stephens. The Petaluma Area

ORIGINAL EGG BASKET, 1918. BERT KERRIGAN, PUBLICIST, STANDS DIRECTLY TO ITS LEFT

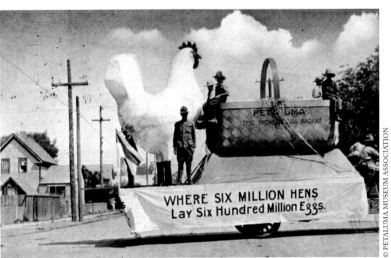

GIANT CHICKEN IS ADDED TO BASKET FOR PARADE FLOAT

CHAMBER OF COMMERCE PROMOTIONAL ENVELOPE FOR 1921 EGG DAY AND RODEO

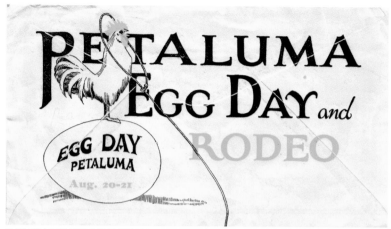

BACK OF PROMOTIONAL ENVELOPE

Chamber of Commerce even issued a multi-colored envelope promoting that year's Egg Day and Rodeo with the cowboy's lasso encircling the chicken on the back of the envelope. Its 1921 brochure — actually almost a book at 60 pages — was an upbeat elegy to the city and its chicken industry, penned, of course, by Kerrigan.

By 1925, Kerrigan had added a bunch of contests to the late August event — best window displays, tastiest egg dish, and a giant tug of war between people from Petaluma and Point Reyes. There was even a free barbecue in the afternoon. All this cost money but the eggs were selling like…well, eggs. A few years later, a giant chicken was added to the egg basket float and it now showed figures of six million hens and 600,000,000 eggs (50,000,000 dozen).

Many of these eggs were sold cooperatively through the Poultry Producers of Central California, formed in 1917. Charles Weeks, quoted before, was an early enthusiast:

"What benefits will the consumer receive from the Association selling their own eggs? The consumer will receive a fresher product direct from the producer. By reason of the Association being able to do a large amount of business at less expense, the consumer should get produce at even less price. The consumer will pay more uniform prices for eggs and not be at the mercy of the speculative element."

Most eggs were sold through the San Francisco Dairy Exchange, but a growing supply soon led to aggressive marketing. One significant and enthusiastic market was New York, where chalk-white eggs were preferred. Its kosher population further insisted upon lemon-yoked eggs, which local ranchers learned how to produce in uniform numbers.

During this period, National Egg Day drew national publicity each year and Petaluma showed up in theater newsreels. By the end of the decade, however, a Kerrigan project to repair the fairground buildings and grandstands had gone far over budget and the Chamber lost faith in him. He would go, and with him went Egg Day celebrations and the famous parades. It was more than 30 years until the parades returned in a modified form as Butter and Egg Days Parades.

A 1928 private photograph of a giant chicken on a basket near the train depot showed that Petaluma's hen population had grown again — to an amazing "Ten Million White Leghorns." Meanwhile, as Petaluma ranchers fed their flocks, hard times were just over the horizon.

LEO BOURKE

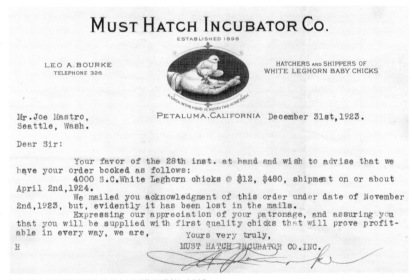

SLOGAN STATIONERY FROM MUST HATCH, 1927

Before relating
the decline in the industry after Wall Street crashed in 1929, another wholly-Petaluma success story is warranted, all about the "World's Largest Baby Chick Hatchery."

On a rainy August day in 1899, Alphonse E. Bourke arrived in Petaluma with his wife and four sons. Informed by a local that there had never been a crop failure here, Bourke was encouraged and decided to put down roots. He started producing his own incubator, which soon became very popular. In 1910, a 320-egg version sold for $35. A hatchery on Seventh Street followed that year with a hatching capacity of 100,000 white leghorns a month.

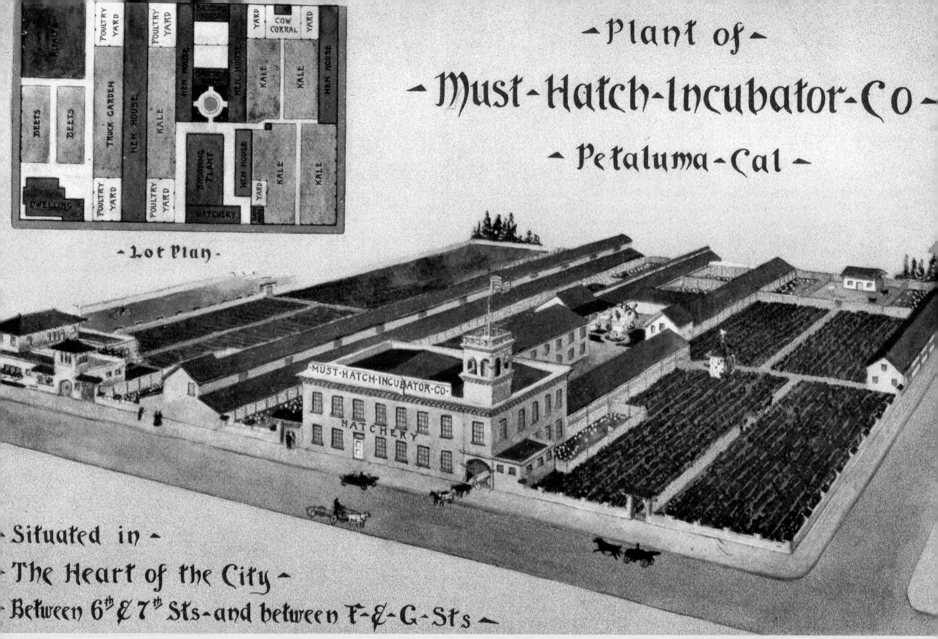

-Plant of-

-Must-Hatch-Incubator-Co-

-Petaluma-Cal-

-Lot Plan-

-Situated in-

The Heart of the City-

-Between 6ᵗʰ & 7ᵗʰ Sts-and between F-&-G-Sts-

MUST HATCH, 1912

"From the garret of a barn to the largest factory and plant in the world is a good reason for six years' time. This is a short story behind this proposition — Merit."

Must Hatch Sales Brochure, circa 1905-10

MUST HATCH EMPLOYEES' PLEDGE

In 1912, Alfonse sold the business to his son Leo. The younger Bourke improved the incubators and the business continued to thrive. An ad on the reverse of a 1912 postcard stated:

"We hatch S.C. White Leghorn chicks and ship them when one day old to points within three days travel by express, from Petaluma. We were the originators of shipping just hatched chicks." (They were fortified by the food in their tiny bodies that could sustain them for up to five days.)

In 1923, when the hatchery had reached a capacity of 600,000 chicks a day, a huge fire destroyed it, but business was too good to give up. By 1927 a new hatchery was ready at 401 Seventh Street, with a significantly larger capacity. Note the company's logo on the invoice from that year — "A Chick in the Hand is Worth Two in the Shell." By 1930, the company could achieve 1,800,000 hatchlings daily and company literature called it the "World's Largest Baby Chick Factory".

Must Hatch, at 500 employees, was probably the largest employer in Petaluma in the early thirties. At that size, the company was large enough to establish a sort of corporate culture and definite esprit de corps. Employees created a flowery "anthem" in praise of the company which attests to that.

One of the most important jobs at Must Hatch was determining the sex of hatchlings, as only pullets were wanted by poultry men. It took three months of full-time training to develop the expertise to gently handle the new chicks and correctly distinguish the females. Eventually the hatchery could promise a 98-99% accuracy in sexing the hatchlings.

The fate of the young pullets depended upon the rancher's goal. If the hens were dedicated to laying eggs for a hatchery, they became free range chickens, getting plenty of scratching and pecking time outside. The industrial hens, producing eggs for the public, were closely penned, fed and handled intensively. Chickens allowed natural conditions could live to four or five years, while factory chickens went to the stew pot at only two or three.

In 1935, Paul Sales, whose own hatchery suffered a bad fire in 1932, joined forces with Leo Bourke to form a successor company at the same location — Sales and Bourke. Although the Depression years were tough on the chicken industry in the 1930s, the company continued to be successful. Ultimately the company was sold to H&N Farms but the hatchery remained open until 1989.

CHAMBER OF COMMERCE BROCHURE
FROM CIRCA 1932 PORTRAYS
AFFLUENT-LOOKING COUPLE
FACING PAGE: VARIOUS GIANT EGG
BASKETS DISPLAYED AT TIMES IN
PETALUMA IN THE 1920'S-40'S

The front and back of a Chamber of Commerce brochure from circa 1932 showed a prosperous-looking family and omnipresent white leghorn flock, but the Kerrigan years of super-hype were over. The clarion call was still evident but in a more minor key, except for the final warranty:

"Petaluma, with its sandy soil, mild climate and excellent marketing and transportation facilities, is the logical place to engage in the poultry industry. Petaluma also enjoys the advantage of having all industries allied with poultry raising in its midst, the result being that feed and supplies are always at hand at a reasonable price. Free consultation and advice is given the poultry men by the service men of the feed dealers, hatcheries and farm bureau. This is very helpful to the beginner and practically insures his success."

"The Petaluma Valley bristles to the number of 5,000,000 [hens], according to the best current estimates, nearly all of them White Leghorns. Before the depression it boasted an even larger poultry population, but with low egg prices many poultry men reduced the size of their flocks."

California Magazine of Pacific Business, 1937

Indeed, the 1930s were tough on Petaluma's chicken ranchers. Egg prices dipped precipitously, never exceeding 22 cents a dozen and dropping to just 19 cents a dozen by 1940. The total chicken population was between five and six million at the end of the decade, and, according to author Thea Lowry, egg production was only about 30 million dozen.

Ironically, Petaluma had constructed a series of giant egg baskets starting in the late 1920s, some with SCWL hens, promoting the industry to tourists. Several of these were present in the 1930s but reflected more affluent days with chicken populations and egg production figures from the 1920s. A chicken basket with eggs (sans chicken) was featured in a 1939 edition of *National Geographic Magazine*, and continued on display into the 1940s.

The 1937 *California* magazine spoke about the increasing production costs for Petaluma poultrymen, especially feed. Economists had even worked out an "egg-feed ratio" — the number of dozens of eggs to purchase 100 pounds of feed. This ratio was 7.07 for 1936 and already at up to 7.73 in early 1937. Labor and land costs were up also. This led to many foreclosures although feed mills extended as much credit as possible.

The Poultry Producers of Central California, the cooperative that had been started decades earlier, was still an active concern at the end of the decade with 400 employees, candling, weighing and shipping eggs all over the country from Petaluma. It sold feed to the ranchers at below market costs during this troubling decade — so most ancillary businesses were doing all they could to support a flagging industry.

Our country was slowly coming out of the Depression as World War II approached, with unemployment down to "only" 9.5 percent by 1941. With the tragedy of the war, though, came an economic upswing so that by 1944 the unemployment rate was only 1.2 percent. In response to rationing (including red meat) the government encouraged increased production of farm products; for example, the Secretary of Agriculture, Claude Wickard, set a goal of an increase of 13 percent in egg production for 1942 alone. Domestic consumption rose from an average of 325 eggs per person pre-war to an all-time high of 390 towards the end of the war — that meant the average man, woman, and child ate one egg or more every day!

Petaluma was equipped to deal with the new demands that resulted from the war and egg production rose accordingly, to a high of 52,415,000 dozen by 1945, when Petaluma ranchers were getting 58 cents a dozen — three times what they got in 1940! At that point the Poultry Producers had 425 employees here. After the war, demand would start to wane. Egg production fell to 43,357,000 dozen by 1954. Per-capita consumption fell to 321 eggs by 1960 (and just 234 eggs by 1990 with the cholesterol scare being a factor).

By the time Petaluma celebrated its Centennial in 1958 with the "World's Egg Basket" slogan still prominently used during the celebration, the downturn was evident. With egg prices up so much since 1940, why was the basket splitting at its seams?

© PETALUMA MUSEUM ASSOCIATION

CHICKEN PHARMACY ON MAIN STREET, DOWNTOWN PETALUMA

The population of Petaluma was 14,000 in 1960. Thirty years later it was three times that at over 43,000. While in 1915 land sold at $450 an acre, by 1976 it was worth as much as $6,000! Rural Petaluma had truly become urban and commuters far outnumbered ranchers, although agriculture continued to be important. "The Indiana/Ohio/Pennsylvania region is the new 'U.S. Egg Basket'," reported the University of California towards the end of this era.

"…average profits for producers since 1966 have averaged less than one cent per dozen. Losses in the 1987-88 period were estimated at $2.45 per hen in California. Everyone has an opinion as to why the industry is in such bad shape. These include: industry expansion, decreasing demand for eggs, tax laws, foreign investors, flock recycling, high flock productivity, and on and on."

An *Egg Economics Update*, University of California, 1989

"Chicken Lady Wanted: Must dress up like a hen, cluck greeting to Petaluma newcomers. No experience needed, but prefer woman who will put civic interest ahead of personal life."

Ad placed in the *San Francisco Chronicle* in 1971 by Chamber of Commerce and found by Bill Pronzini

Wire cages suspended from a ceiling and conveyer belts made clean-up and egg collection easier but changing to this type of chicken farming was expensive, and the price ranchers were getting for their eggs could not cover such expenses. Farms in Southern California and the South had become modernized and held gigantic flocks. Also, chicken farmers had never received government subsidies to support prices, and many of the general public now ate cereal for breakfast — not eggs.

Additionally, while in the past many children had taken over their parents' ranches, postwar generations sought more formal education and an easier life compared to the dawn to dusk drudgery of operating a chicken farm.

Another critical blow in this era was the failure of the Poultry Producers of Central California, through which many local ranchers sold their eggs, and a large employer here. They went bankrupt in 1964, taking with them millions of dollars that members (some of them small farmers) had invested.

Even Petaluma's famous chicken pharmacy — opened in the 1920s to help ranchers fight poultry diseases — closed in the late 1950s, leaving its long-term occupancy downtown on Main Street (now Petaluma Boulevard).

Where once egg producers had numbered in the thousands, there were only 300 by the end of the 1980s. Even the "World's Largest Baby Chick Hatchery" could not make it anymore and closed in 1989.

Although Petaluma picture postcards would still show leghorns, the "Egg Basket of the World" days were over.

PICTURE POSTCARD, PROBABLY FROM THE 1970S-80S

ALLEN SHAINSKY, WHO FOUNDED
PETALUMA POULTRY PROCESSORS

PETALUMA POULTRY PRODUCTS

By 2007, California was no longer first in egg production in the U.S, with fewer than five billion eggs produced, the smallest number since 1959. In fact, the state has became an egg importer since 1991. High production costs are to blame. Sales here now are for eggs and broilers — gone are the days when there was a market for stewing chickens.

An interesting trend is developing with consumers more concerned than ever with how animals are raised. "Free range" is the byword now and healthy products have helped the fortunes of two current Petaluma companies, Petaluma Poultry Processors and Petaluma Farms.

Early in the 20th century, Eastern European Jews were attracted to rural Sonoma County and especially the Petaluma area in what author Thea Lowry described as a "back-to-the-land movement" for those tired of urban settings. By 1930 there were 300 Jewish families farming here. One of these families was that of Russian immigrant Israel Shainsky, who arrived around 1920 and raised chickens. His son, Allen Shainsky, would found Petaluma Poultry 50 years later.

> "Petaluma has survived as a significant egg production region in California. Petaluma is a paradigm of the American poultry industries. As such it has experienced cultural changes and revolutions before the rest of rural America."

F.A. Bradley, 2000

DARREL FREITAS, PRESIDENT OF PETALUMA POULTRY

It was in 1986 that Petaluma Poultry produced its breakthrough product — Rocky, the Free-Range Chicken. Raised on a soft bed of rice hulls, the chickens were allowed to roam freely in the poultry house and in a small outside pen. Consumers found that such "natural" chickens — with no preservatives or any other synthetic ingredients — were good tasting and of high quality.

In 1989, "Rosie" became the first chicken certified as "organic" by the ASDA. Rosie is fed soy-based organic food — and even the soil upon which she treads must be free of pesticides. Several years later, a smaller, young version of Rocky was created — Rocky Junior. The Petaluma Poultry brands have high product loyalty, especially in California, Oregon and Washington.

Allen Shainsky died in 2000. Two years later, Petaluma Poultry was bought by Coleman Natural Foods, LLC, headquartered in Golden, Colorado. Petaluma Poultry's sales continue to grow year after year, now approaching $100 million. The company processes 14,000,000 chickens annually, with the majority of them coming from Sonoma County farms. With 330 employees, it is one of Petaluma's largest employers.

Darrel Freitas joined the company when it opened in 1971, at the age of 19. His first job was catching chickens. Now he's the company's president. Freitas says:

> "I've worked for Petaluma [Poultry] for 36 years, and really have enjoyed working with Allen and all the local people, and now we have the next generation of local kids working with us. The agriculture business is still good in Petaluma. We have a long-term commitment to the community and will keep going with our business."

Steve Mahrt is the owner and founder of Petaluma Farms. He estimates there are still a million laying chickens in Sonoma County and that two-thirds of them are in the Petaluma area. Mahrt says there are only three commercial egg producers left and his is the only independently-owned business.

Petaluma Farms now sells about 156,000 dozen eggs a year, and even maintains a retail outlet in town — Skippy's Egg Shoppe. Steve is a third generation Petaluma egg farmer, so he has been around chickens all his life. He maintains free range flocks of Single-Comb White Leghorns and Rhode Island Reds.

Mahrt opened Petaluma Farms in 1983. The Rhode Island Reds were responsible for one of his earlier products — Rock Island Fertile Eggs, which are brown eggs, by the way. In 1996 he marketed organic eggs, certified by OCIA (Organic Crop Improvement Association). This was followed in 1999 by another healthy product, DHA Omega-3 eggs. DHA Omega-3 is a long-chain fatty acid which "is vital for a healthy heart and for brain and eye development and functions" according to the carton's label. These eggs also have six times more Vitamin E than normal eggs. The chickens that produce these eggs have algae in their diet.

As to the future of Petaluma Farms, Mahrt says the chicken business is still largely "generational". Years ago, he points out, children often took over the business from parents but that is no longer common practice, given the draw of colleges and larger urban centers. As of today, Petaluma Farms is very successful, and Mahrt does not appear ready to retire or step aside.

Although Petaluma is no longer heralded as the "Egg Basket of the World" and the Chamber no longer staffs a "chicken lady", many reminders of those days linger: fallen chicken houses on the rural fringes of town, reflections of bygone days on public murals, and even surviving buildings. Still standing, for example, is the 180-foot grain elevator building that housed the Poultry Producers as late as 1960 — and Must Hatch's classic building at Seventh and F Streets.

Bert Kerrigan's final words in his 70-page Chamber booklet of almost 90 years ago still ring true today, whether one is involved in the chicken business or not:

> "Taking it all in all, Petaluma is a place where a man [or woman] can make money, have an interesting vocation, a good home and enjoy life. Not too far removed from San Francisco, he has every advantage that mankind provides and nature produces."

STEVE MAHRT, OWNER OF PETALUMA FARMS

GRAIN ELEVATORS, FORMERLY OWNED BY POULTRY PRODUCERS, NOW OWNED BY DAIRYMEN'S

EIGHT

PETALUMA'S LASTING BUSINESSES
by Vern Piccinotti

The stories of this baker's dozen of Petaluma's oldest companies are testimony to our city's ability to adapt to the future while retaining the best of the past.

The Petaluma Argus-Courier

The newspaper traces its earliest origins to the *Petaluma Weekly Journal* and *Sonoma County Advertiser*, which appeared on August 15, 1855, published by Thomas L. Thompson. On April 26, 1856, Thompson sold the paper to Henry L. Weston. After shortening the title to *Sonoma County Journal*, Weston merged the paper with the *Petaluma Argus* on February 25, 1864, creating the *Petaluma Journal and Argus*. The last vestiges of the *Journal* disappeared in 1873 when the paper became the *Petaluma Weekly Argus*.

In 1900, Jesse Doud Olmsted of Gallipolis, Ohio, purchased an interest in the *Argus*, beginning a 65-year association with the publication that eventually involved his sons, grandsons, and other descendants.

On January 1, 1928, the *Argus* acquired the *Courier* and the combined *Argus-Courier* made its appearance in July of that year. In 1965, the Olmsted family sold the paper to the Scripps League, which, in 1996, sold to Pulitzer interests. The *Argus-Courier* was acquired by the *New York Times* Publishing Company in 2001 and was converted to a weekly.

The history of the paper includes a labyrinth of owners, titles, and printing schedules — weekly, daily, morning and evening. Through it all, the succession of newpapers has continued to publish.

By the way, special editions of the *Argus-Courier* are primary sources of Petaluma history. These include the 1941 85th Anniversary Edition, the paper's Centennial edition in August, 1955, and the Petaluma (City) Centennial editions in 1958.

The *Argus-Courier* and its antecedents miss holding the title of "Oldest Continuing Business in Petaluma" by less than a year.

Parent-Sorensen Mortuary

A result of the merger of Parent Funeral Chapel and the Sorensen Funeral Home, this entity traces its origins to the 1856 mortuary founded by Charles Blackburn at Third (now Petaluma Boulevard South) and B Streets. In 1890, Charles Blackburn turned the business over to his son, John S. Blackburn, who was joined in 1903 by his brother, Frank L. Blackburn. John died in 1903.

TERRY SMITH

John C. Mount acquired a half-interest in the business in 1908 and the remaining Blackburn interest in 1915. The business was then known as the John C. Mount Funeral Chapel and was relocated to 216 Washington Street in 1921.

Art Parent, later mayor of Petaluma, joined Mount on August 1, 1938, and purchased Mount's interest on May 1, 1944. The business was thereafter known as Parent Funeral Chapel. In September 1965, the company was relocated to a new building at 850 Keokuk Street. An initial interest in this chapel was acquired in 1977 by James Smith and Martin "Buzz" Rodgers, who purchased the remaining interest in August 1981.

Sorensen Funeral Home, located at 400 Washington Street, was founded in 1925 by William Sorensen. In 1939, Sorensen purchased the ornate home of Dennis J. Healey at Washington and Keokuk Streets and moved his funeral home into it. Oscar Pope became the manager and, with son Robert Pope, operated it following the death of Sorensen in 1955. They built and occupied the building currently housing the Petaluma Police Department on Petaluma Boulevard North and Cemetery Road in 1969.

James Smith and Martin "Buzz" Rodgers acquired the business of Sorensen Funeral Home in June of 1982, and the Parent and Sorensen entities were combined as Parent-Sorensen Mortuary at 850 Keokuk Street.

The Washoe House

Although located some five miles northwest of Petaluma, this site has been an integral part of the town's history. It was called Stony Point House when it was founded as a stagecoach stop and hostelry by William Ayres in 1859. The land was owned by Augustus J. Bowie, a successful Washoe County (Nevada) miner — and that's almost

certainly the reason for the name we know today.

At that time, though, the area was a village called Stony Point. A post office existed there as early as April 13, 1857, with several other businesses listed in 1859 and 1860.

Legend, oft repeated but never substantiated, maintains that infamous stagecoach robber, Black Bart (aka Charles E. Boles) and General Ulysses S. Grant were guests of the establishment. Boles' presence, while clearly possible due to his likely special interest in the schedules of the three stage lines which stopped there, cannot be substantiated. No known visit by Grant is documented after he gained prominence — though he did make a brief trip to the area in 1879 after leaving the presidency.

Ownership of the Washoe House eventually passed to the Wilson family, who operated the surrounding ranch and adjacent rock quarry into the 1950s — with the Washoe House as their residence.

Washoe House was purchased from the Wilson estate by Tony Andresen in 1951. He remodeled and operated it as a restaurant and tavern until his death in 1971. It was then purchased by Bill Drew and two partners. In April 1974, Drew and wife Edith became sole owners. The Drew family presently operates the enterprise.

Local papers reported during the Civil War that a contingent of Northern supporters from Petaluma — apparently including members of the Hewston Guard, a local militia unit — proceeded toward Santa Rosa, vowing to attack a "Copperhead" pro-Southern newspaper there.

On the way, they stopped at the Washoe House for refreshment. As the story is told, the spirit of the mission to Santa Rosa was soon overcome by the spirits served at the Washoe House and the mission was terminated. It is not known to have been rescheduled.

In its first known advertisement, appearing in the *Sonoma County Journal*, July 13, 1860, Washoe House pledged to meet "all reasonable demands of man and beast."

MARIN FRENCH CHEESE COMPANY

The Marin French Cheese Company was founded by Jefferson A. Thompson, a native of Illinois, where he had learned to make cheddar cheese. Arriving in California by 1860, Thompson purchased the 700-acre ranch on which the current cheese factory is located in 1865 and began to make cheese for the San Francisco market. The factory's continuous production since that time lends support to their assertion that it is the oldest continuously operating cheese factory in the United States.

At the turn of the century, with a cheese factory and curing cellars established, Thompson began producing the Camembert for which the company became widely known. The factory has been successively operated and managed by Jefferson A. Thompson's sons, Rudolph and Jefferson T. Thompson and their sons, Pierce, Douglas and Ed Thompson, in addition to other family members. The three Thompson generations represent more than 130 years of operation.

The 1912 incorporation of the company formally established the Marin French Cheese Company.

Early company brand names included "Tocoloma" and "Yellow Buck". However, Marin French Cheese Company is best known for its "Rouge et Noir" (red and black) label Camembert.

In 1998, the Thompson family sold the company to Jim Boyce, who has expanded its cheese products from the traditional company standards — Schloss, Breakfast Cheese, Fromage de Brie and Camembert — to some 40 varieties for dairy, deli and food service operations nationwide.

Long recognized regionally for its excellence, Marin French is now consistently achieving national and international recognition. In 2006, the company earned 16 awards in the American

Cheese Society International Competition and six medals in the World Cheese Awards Competition.

Marin French Cheese Company — popularly known as "The Cheese Factory" — is located at 7500 Red Hill Road, on Petaluma's D Street Extension. The present retail sales and wrapping rooms are located directly over the original cellars.

CYPRESS HILL MEMORIAL PARK

Cypress Hill was founded in 1866 by John A. McNear. McNear elected to start a cemetery on land he owned when he was unable to locate a suitable burial site for his wife during the winter season. Since then, Cypress Hill has had a succession of owners, including McNear himself, the McNear Company, and a Petaluma investment group headed by Henry Murphy and later owned by George Tomasini. Since 2004, the cemetery has been owned by James Smith and Martin "Buzz" Rodgers of Parent-Sorensen Mortuary.

For 40 years — from about 1881 to about 1921 — James Franklin Penry served as Superintendent of Cypress Hill. He was originally hired by John A. McNear. In 1861, at the age of 15, Penry had been drafted into Company E, 2nd North Carolina Infantry, Confederate States Army. He was captured and imprisoned. Upon release, he joined the Union Army and served with distinction until the end of the Civil War. He arrived in Petaluma in 1881.

James Penry is the great-grandfather of Richard Allen Penry, Petaluma's only recipient of the Congressional Medal of Honor. Richard Penry was decorated for valor during the Viet Nam war. Both are buried in the Penry plot at Cypress Hill.

TERRY SMITH

EXCHANGE BANK

Exchange Bank was founded in Santa Rosa in 1890 by Manville Doyle, who had acquired the Santa Rosa Savings Bank in 1874. Doyle was a native of Sangamon County, Illinois. He came to California during the gold rush and later prospered in dealing cattle and raising racehorses in the Petaluma area.

Manville's son, Frank P. Doyle, was born in Petaluma in 1863 and became President of the bank following his father's death on August 21, 1916. Under the leadership of Frank Doyle, Exchange Bank has become Sonoma County's largest and most influential "homegrown" bank. Through the special interests of Frank P. Doyle, this bank is well known for the "Doyle Scholarship" which has provided millions of dollars for attendance of Sonoma County students at Santa Rosa Junior College. More than $20 million in scholarships has been awarded to more than 40,000 Sonoma County recipients. The bank has had a Petaluma presence for several decades.

Frank P. Doyle was a foremost leader in marshalling Northern California support for construction of the Golden Gate Bridge and was a passenger in the first automobile to cross the bridge on the day of its opening.

LACE HOUSE LINEN SUPPLY, INC.

Established in 1901 by Jean Momboisse, this business was known for some 60 years as Lace House Laundry prior to becoming a linen supply service. It has long been identified with the Libarle family and Lucien "Red" Libarle who was born in 1908.

After graduating from Petaluma High School, Lucien worked in the family laundry. In 1939, he married Emily "Milli" Benedetti, sister of Gene Benedetti, the future manager of the Petaluma Co-operative Creamery, head coach of the legendary Petaluma Leghorns semi-pro football team, and later founder of Clover Stornetta Farms.

When the laundry burned to the ground in 1947, Lucien's family elected not to rebuild. However, Lucien went ahead on his own and, in 1948, reopened Lace House Laundry in its new facility on Liberty Street. Following college and military service, Lucien's son Daniel became affiliated with the company. In 1973, Daniel entered into an agreement to buy the company from Lucien and has been sole owner since 1997. It has operated from an expanded modern facility on Lindbergh Lane since 2004.

In addition to owning and operating Lace House Linen Supply, Dan Libarle is a prominent civic leader. He was founder and Chairman

of the Bank of Petaluma upon its organization in 1997 and is a board member of Greater Bay Bank Corp, which merged with the Bank of Petaluma in October, 2000.

Van Bebber Brothers

THE KAMP'S LIVERY BUILDING LATER BECAME VAN BEBBER BROTHERS

Founded in November, 1901, by George W. Van Bebber and Fred E. Van Bebber as a blacksmith shop, Van Bebber Brothers is the oldest business in Petaluma that has been owned and managed by the same family since its inception. Through five generations, the company successfully transitioned from blacksmithing operations located on East Washington Street into automotive repair and machine shop services. Today, they specialize in steel fabrication and distribution.

In 1918, the company moved to a site at 246 Main Street (now Petaluma Boulevard) with George W. Van Bebber buying the interest of Fred E. Van Bebber the following year. In 1925, George E. "Ellie" Van Bebber and Alvin Van Bebber (sons of George W.) became the second generation of management. Alvin, a Stanford-educated engineer, was killed in a hit-and-run accident in 1951. Co-founder George W. Van Bebber died in 1958 and George E. "Ellie" Van Bebber died in 1999.

In 1949, Royce L. Van Bebber (the son of George E. "Ellie" Van Bebber) joined the company. In 1956, the business relocated to a larger building at 729 Petaluma Boulevard South (then known as Third Street). The machine shop business was sold in 1969 and — in 1971 — certain retail aspects of the business were sold. Emphasis was thereafter placed on the sale and distribution of steel and related value-added services.

Rick Van Bebber (son of Royce L.) joined the company in 1973 and currently serves as President. His son, Royce R. Van Bebber, who represents the family's fifth generation, joined the company in 1997 and serves as Supervisor of Daily Operations.

At its Centennial observance in 2001, Chairman Royce L. Van Bebber observed that Van Bebber Brothers moves forward into its second century of business with optimism and enthusiasm — confidently relying upon a combination of established experience and youthful exuberance.

Rex Hardware

Rex Hardware was founded in 1907 by Ernest Hobbie, Park Van Bebber and Herbert Sweed. Hobbie later purchased the interests of his partners. George Hobbie, the son of Ernest Hobbie, began management of the store in 1930. Later, George and brother Walter Hobbie purchased the business from their mother, Hannah Hobbie. George Hobbie served in World War II as an aide to Pacific Fleet Admiral Chester W. Nimitz.

In 1942, when Rex Hardware was located on the northwest corner of B and then Main Street, across the street from its current location, the store was destroyed by fire. It re-opened in a larger space across the street, at the southeast corner of B and Fourth Streets.

REX HARDWARE FIRE, 1942

Rex Hardware was purchased from the Hobbie family by Henry Tomasini, Petaluma banker and nephew of prominent early hardware merchant, A. F. Tomasini. The business is currently operated by Henry's son, Jeff Tomasini. Rex burned again in 2006, but reopened at the same location in mid-2007 following construction of a building that retains much of the character of the century-old structure it replaces.

REX HARDWARE REOPENS, AFTER 2006 FIRE, AUGUST 2007

Miller, operating as Kresky Manufacturing Company, expanded into the building of residential furnaces. Kresky's oil-fired floor furnace was the first to be marketed by any firm in the oil heating industry. During World War II, Kresky products were used extensively by both land and naval forces in a variety of applications.

In 1951, Kresky expanded into the high quality metal sign business. Kresky Signs was incorporated in 1953 as a separate division of Kresky Manufacturing Company. In 1958, Clarence Miller died and was succeeded as president by his son, Craig Miller. The company expanded by buying two other oil burner businesses. During the 1960s, the company also built business machine and early computer cabinets for Ampex and IBM.

In 1969, Kresky Manufacturing Company was sold to Zero Manufacturing of Burbank, California, and in 1971, operations were moved to Southern California. Kresky Signs was re-incorporated in recognition of the sale of its parent company. The president of Kresky Signs, Inc., is now Craig Miller, Jr., who represents the third generation of the family to operate the business.

KRESKY SIGNS, INC.

Kresky Signs was founded in 1910 by Jesse E. Kresky, who migrated from Minnesota to Petaluma to study the chicken business and its equipment. Kresky had an early interest in improving chicken incubating and brooding equipment and was convinced that oil heating was a safe, efficient, and economical source of heat for hatching and raising chicks. His invention, the Kresky Automatic Brooder Stove, employed his concepts. Kresky was soon inundated with orders for the stove from farmers. Bootleggers were also reported to value the soot-free oil burners which were safer than earlier models. It's also interesting to note that illegal stills could easily be concealed in the burners. Kresky started his company in 1910 in his garage but soon required additional space.

In 1938, Kresky sold the business to Clarence A. Miller, who had come to Petaluma in response to an ad for a steamboat purser. He briefly served as purser on the famed Steamer Gold on the Petaluma River, but left the river to become the sole distributor of Standard Oil products in the Petaluma area.

PETALUMA CO-OPERATIVE CREAMERY

Incorporated September 12, 1913, the Petaluma Co-operative Creamery was a success from the beginning. Under the leadership of George Dondero, a prominent and visionary dairy industry leader, the co-op was soon shipping a variety of dairy products throughout

Northern California and providing a sound and reliable local market for area milk producers.

In 1946, following his service in the U.S. Navy, Gene Benedetti was hired by Dondero as a field representative to establish liaison with local farmers. Dondero, an ardent sports fan, also supported Benedetti's leadership role in organizing and coaching the Petaluma Leghorns, a semi-professional football team which became a regional dynasty between 1946 and 1958. The creamery provided employment opportunities for many of the players in the period between the end of World War II and the emergence of the National Football League.

In 1955, Benedetti succeeded Dondero as General Manager of the Co-op, which by now was a major Northern California force in dairy processing and product distribution.

In the early 1970s, the board of the co-op dropped the name "Petaluma" from the title of the business — thereafter being known as the California Co-operative Creamery. On August 22, 1975, the Creamery suffered a fire that destroyed its bottling plant but spared the processing portion of the facility. Faced with an estimated cost of $4 million to replace the bottling plant, the board, in the summer of 1977, made the decision to sell its distribution rights to Benedetti and a group of investors. Its well-established "Clover" brand went with those rights.

Benedetti and his co-investors later purchased the Stornetta Brothers Dairy of Sonoma and founded Clover-Stornetta Farms. Thereafter, California Co-operative Creamery became less important. It was sold to California Gold, which in turn was sold to the Dairy Farmers of America. The Creamery was purchased by Spring Hill Jersey Cheese in 2005 and continues as a cheese production and processing facility.

Clover-Stornetta is the successor of Petaluma Co-operative Creamery and still markets its flagship "Clover" line of dairy products.

HUNT & BEHRENS, INC.

Hunt & Behrens, Inc., was organized in 1921 as a partnership between Marvin Hunt, who at the age of 15 in 1892 had gone to work for G. P. McNear Co., and Carl N. Behrens. Hunt and Behrens early recognized the advantages and nutritional superiority of scientifically formulated poultry and dairy feeds and built their company around this concept — serving the rapidly growing agricultural community in and around Petaluma and throughout Northern California.

The company's original mill was located at First and C Streets, with a retail outlet located in the building on Keller Street which was later occupied by Weller-Hopkins Furniture and Tuttle Drug Store. That building now houses Pazzo restaurant.

Following World War II, Hunt & Behrens built the current mill at 30 Lakeville Street, allowing the consolidation of manufacturing and retail sales at one site. Hunt retired in 1947 and died the following year.

TERRY SMITH

The Hunt interests were acquired by Behrens and in 1948 the former partnership was incorporated as Hunt & Behrens, Inc.

Ed Behrens, son of Carl N. Behrens, joined the company in August, 1945. He retired as Chief Executive Officer in 1997 but maintains an active interest in the company.

Today, Hunt & Behrens, Inc. continues to serve the agricultural needs of the area through the manufacture and supply of mixed feeds, hay, grain and pharmaceuticals. The company is currently under the management of owners Dan J. Figone, Robert J. Falco and Joseph H. Masciorini.

VOLPI'S RISTORANTE
AND OLD WORLD BAR

On February 12, 1925, Silvio and Mary Volpi purchased the turn-of-the-century building at Kentucky and Washington Streets that had been owned by Louis Solari since 1908. There, the Volpi family established an Italian market, deli, and bar.

Volpi's has been famous throughout its history for its "backroom" bar and community meeting place. This location became widely known during the 1950s as the site of the "Petaluma Press Club" — where employees of the *Petaluma Argus-Courier* used to gather after work. It was also the unofficial headquarters of famed Petaluma personality and "peopleologist" Bill Soberanes.

During Prohibition, Volpi's was renowned as a "speakeasy." The backroom served local "product" — manufactured nearby, but not on premises — to patrons who were awaiting their grocery orders. Many a younger Petaluman of an earlier era will recall being told to wait outside while Dad went to the back "to get the weather report."

Following the death of Silvio Volpi in 1956 and Mary Volpi in 1979, Volpi's continued as a grocery and deli until the business was converted in 1992 into a restaurant — now operated by John Volpi and his wife, Mary Lee Volpi. John and his sister, Sylvia, provide accordion music for the entertainment of patrons. Volpi's has become regionally famous for the quality and diversity of its Italian cuisine.

Volpi's is unique in that it is the oldest Petaluma business operating in its original location. It is reputed that Volpi's and Andresen's — both in Petaluma — were granted two of the first three liquor licenses in California.

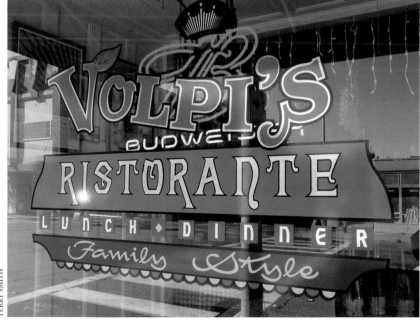

NINE

Petaluma Neighborhoods a Half-Century Ago
by JoAnn Ritko Pozzi

Lund's Drive-In Restaurant, where carhops delivered a little aluminum tray that clamped to your car…was the place where teens got a cherry or chocolate Coke®…

© PETALUMA MUSEUM ASSOCIATION

RAMP AT BACK OF PETALUMA GENERAL HOSPITAL

© PETALUMA MUSEUM ASSOCIATION

PETALUMA GENERAL HOSPITAL

SoBe is a district that is defined and named by me, that ran south from B Street to I Street — between Main Street (now Petaluma Boulevard South) and First Street.

It started at Lund's Drive-In Restaurant, where carhops delivered little aluminum trays that clamped on the side of your car. In the '50s, that was the place where teens got a cherry or chocolate Coke® in a real glass — or a burger and French fries, if they really had some cash.

The district I define starts there because — when we cruised Main Street — that's where we checked out who was out, and that's where we turned around to go back down to Washington. Of course, that was before the bowling alley down by the Vet's Memorial was built.

Petaluma General Hospital was at Sixth and I Streets — two Victorian Houses connected by a series of ramps. It was run by Jo Millmister and financed by some local doctors. It was the only hospital we knew then. Hillcrest and Petaluma Valley Hospitals came much later.

Across from Lund's (which is now Bundesen Realty) was (and is) the Buckhorn Bar. It is one of three bars in town that have old-style liquor licenses that allow OFF sale liquor to be consumed ON the premises. In those days, they also sold abalone to their customers — about 500 per season for $1.50 apiece.

At the corner of Second and G, where the Quilted Angel is now, was the Coca Cola bottling plant. During Prohibition, Petaluma Soda and Sarsaparilla was across the street — and had a bootleg operation. The reason I know some of these things is that, in the '60s, I worked in the neighborhood.

Across from Rivertown Feed was the McKinney Livery Stable that's now out on McNear Peninsula. It was next to the Fire House designed by Brainerd Jones. Roughly where the entrance to the new parking garage on C Street is today was the exit from Small's Scales — so there were trucks all around, all the time.

In fact, the whole area was bustling with the transportation of products in and out of Petaluma. Among the goods in transit were hay, cows, milk, sheep, eggs, chickens, ducks, dirt, gravel and asphalt. Trains still hauled commodities on the tracks that ran behind the scales.

Many young people, in those days, had jobs lumping hay and working in construction, as well as at businesses like the Heinz Brothers Rock Quarry. Soon that location, at the south end of

MCKINNEY LIVERY STABLE

MAIN STREET FROM PENRY PARK

Petaluma Boulevard below the Petaluma Golf & Country Club, will be a neighborhood of 100 new homes.

Behind the McKinney Livery Stable was a "house of ill repute" which, I'm told, was a Victorian house with a climbing rose bush on it. When the house was to be torn down — so the story goes — Emily Gale's mother-in-law bought it, dismantled it, and hauled the house out to her place on Red Hill Road. It's my understanding that it's still there, in the grass up in the corner. It's also said that two "prominent men in agriculture" had the rose bush that had adorned the "house of ill repute" moved to the Small's scale house — in memory of the good times they and their friends had at that establishment. When the scale house was moved, it's said that — as a condition of the permits to build the parking garage that replaced it — the developer was required to incorporate the rose bush into the landscaping somewhere in the Theater Square area.

Later, two women were concerned about the sickly condition of the bush and decided its location was not suitable. They petitioned for custody so the bush could be better cared for — and the city granted custody to the Petaluma Library and Historical Museum.

NoWa is another District I've defined myself. It was the area on and around Main Street (now Petaluma Boulevard North) from Washington Street north to Bridge Street (now an extension of Lakeville Street).

The real name of the grocery we children called "Chinamen's Market" was Petaluma Grocery. It was owned by several Chinese families and political correctness was not what it is today — especially among 8-year-olds.

Over on Bridge Street at the end of Madison was the Clover Stornetta plant — originally Reif and Brody and later Petaluma Poultry Processors. They processed kosher chickens one day a week and Chinese-style chickens (with the heads and feet still attached) on a regular schedule as well.

A low, flat-topped building called the Green House was across the street, and if the red light was on we all knew the girls were working. The chief of police had a back route to the establishment across a foot bridge from Poultry Alley. That's where Dairymen's Feed is now, but back then it was Poultry Producers and Nulaid Egg.

The place was raided from time to time, but no one was ever arrested. It was common knowledge that a phone call was made to tip off the patrons before a raid. Rumor has it that the customers would hang out somewhere like the 101 Club until another call came in to tell them that the coast was clear.

Next to the Petaluma Grocery was Chandler's Dairy. The treat for us was to have a grilled cheese sandwich and some maple nut ice cream.

Next down the block, at 501 Main where Vanda Floral Design is now, was Ed Gerrit's Richfield gas station. Gerrit's was the first place my parents had a charge account. I still have a receipt for 9 gallons of gas for $1.71. That's just 19 cents a gallon.

Over one block, at the corner of Kent and Kentucky Streets next to Poehlman's Hatchery, is a house that was ordered from a Sears Roebuck catalogue. It was shipped on a flat car and assembled in place — two stories with a half basement and a garage tucked under the Kent Street side. It stands there today, now painted a brick color.

Back on what was Main Street — at 300 and 304 at the crest of the hill — is a double front brick building that was the overalls factory. They had three shifts of workers each day and nearly 40 women sewing overalls on non-motorized, foot-treadle machines. Two of my aunts worked there.

A block west of Main, on Washington Street, is the Hotel Petaluma. It was "state-of-the-art" when it was built in 1923. The area that was converted to a bar (when the Elks Club owned it) was once a courtyard with lush foliage, a brick fishpond, and seating for lounging. On one side of the courtyard, there were large glass windows and a door leading to the lobby. The registration desk was at the foot of the stairs on the right. The hotel had an elegant restaurant as well. If a young man asked a young woman to accompany him to dinner at the Redwood Room, I'm told you knew it was serious.

LEFT: EGG QUEEN RUTH SJOSTON AND BIG CHIEF WHITE HORSE EAGLE IN THE ENTRANCE COURTYARD OF THE HOTEL PETALUMA

RIGHT: THE REDWOOD ROOM OF THE HOTEL PETALUMA

BELOW: THE PETALUMA GROCERY AT 605 MAIN STREET WAS THE LARGEST SUPERMARKET IN NORTHERN CALIFORNIA

ANDRESEN'S TAVERN

THE LESSON IN THE CEILING
OF ANDRESEN'S TAVERN

In 1934, Hank and Hans Andresen's Tavern was in a slightly different location on Western Avenue — on the same side of the street but under the Continental Hotel on the corner of Kentucky Street. There were retail shops under the back of that hotel and, when you walked by the front, you had to look up to see the people in the lobby. Next door, where Preferred Sonoma Caterers is today, was the Stratford Theater — at one time a silent movie house.

In the '60s, the hotel burned to the ground. It smoldered for days. Everyone was very upset at the loss, although there were certainly other hotels in town. Before the fire, though, the father and son who owned Andresen's Tavern reopened at 19 Western Avenue, where it is today — still operated by a family member.

I don't know how long ago the collection of guns and animal heads was started. There are "jackalope," moose, gazelle, and buffalo. There's even some kind of pig. About twice a year the bar is closed for a couple of days. The collection comes down for cleaning, as does the inventory on the back bar. The walls and mirrors are cleaned as well. Some are cleaned with soap and water, but all the animal heads get a bath in club soda. If you happened to be there during the cleaning, you'd probably notice the hole in the ceiling and ask about the rubber chicken that hangs through it. That's when you'd learn "The lesson in the ceiling of Andresen's Tavern."

At one of the times when the collection was down, an Andresen sister happened to be up on a ladder. Her brother had one of the rifles in his hand. No one had ever noticed, in all the times the guns were up and down, that any of them were loaded. This one was. The gun went off, just barely missing the sister's head, and blew a hole in the ceiling.

Most business owners would have covered that hole immediately and painted it quickly to match — but not in Petaluma. The owners of Andresen's saw it as a way to remember a very important lesson. They left the hole, climbed up into the loft, and dropped a symbolic Petaluma rubber chicken through it. Anyone who has asked since then has learned the lesson: When handling a firearm, never assume it is not loaded.

CONTINENTAL HOTEL FIRE, MAY 5, 1968

In the '60s, the [Continental] hotel burned to the ground.
It smoldered for days. Everyone was very upset at the loss.

TEN

The Columns of "Mr. Petaluma"
by Bill Soberanes

In his long career, he interviewed, and was photographed with, literally hundreds of international celebrities and local personalities.

BILL SOBERANES (LEFT) WITH FRANK SINATRA

Petaluma newspaper columnist Bill Soberanes was the founder of the International People Meeters/ People Finders Club. In his long career, he interviewed, and was photographed with, literally hundreds of international celebrities and local personalities. He died on June 2, 2003 — exactly 49 years to the day after writing his first column for the *Petaluma Argus-Courier*.

Soberanes was known as "Mr. Petaluma" because of the endless support he showed for his hometown. He was one of the organizers of the World Wrist-Wrestling Championship, for which Petaluma became known around the globe for many years. What follows is just a small sampling of the stories he wrote about the people he met:

THE FIRST COLUMN - JUNE 2, 1954

This being my first column for the *Argus-Courier*, I would like to tell you just what you will be reading in this space. We will tell you about local happenings, about the many people we chance to meet from all walks of life, the famous, the near famous, the characters, and the everyday citizen. We hope to gaze into our crystal ball and predict what will happen from time to time. All in all we hope to give you a variety column that will be of interest to everyone.

Today we will tell you about a Petaluman who has really made good in the sport of kings. Our man of the hour is Emmett Tassi, the third largest breeder of standard-bred horses in the United States. Emmett Tassi is no "Johnny-come-lately" to the sport of harness racing, having owned and raced his first horse, Cookie-T, in his hometown of Petaluma way back in 1917. Old timers will remember Cookie-T as a three-year-old that raced and won at the Pan-Pacific International Exposition in 1915. Last Saturday, Mabel Tassi, driven by owner Emmett Tassi, won the California Harness Horse Breeders Association Free-for-All stakes at Bay Meadows. Immediately after this race, Emmett rushed to Petaluma to help his father celebrate his 80th birthday. The famed Tassi horses will not be at the Sonoma County Fair this year. Instead, Mr. Tassi will take five of his top horses to Yonkers, New York, and then to Long Island where they will face the best trotting horses in America.

A bit of this and that:

While Earle Bond was playing the organ at the Redwood Room of the Hotel Petaluma Saturday night, a couple decided they would dance. To the amazement of everyone present, they both started turning handsprings. We were later told that they were professional dancers taking a busman's holiday.

Those who witnessed the big traffic jam on Petaluma's East Washington Street Saturday morning tell us it was caused by a proud white leghorn rooster casually strolling across this busy street.

DOING THE TOWN
WITH ENTERTAINER JEANNIE McFADDEN

The Petaluma nightclub type of entertainment has changed, and today I'm writing about it and featuring one of the beautiful ladies who was a star.

Back in the 1950s, Bill Fontes ran a couple of entertainment type nightclubs in Petaluma. Bill's first club was located on Petaluma's Main Street. His second was near the railroad tracks in East Petaluma. In those days, they used to say that Bill brought top entertainers in the musical field to Petaluma.

Today's story features Jeannie McFadden, the lady who was not only talented but a glamorous beauty. I remember Fontes describing how the "Stage Door Johnnies" brought bouquets of flowers and boxes of candy to Jeannie. He added, "Her biggest competition in Petaluma entertainment is at the Rose Court — a lady musician who plays and sings there named Annabel Brown."

McFadden was known affectionately as the "Sweetheart of Petaluma," a hometown kind of girl.

On a number of occasions the Villa Fontes and the Rose Court had their entertainers trade places. They used to say it was a contest between Annabel Brown and Jeannie McFadden to see which was the more popular. If you believed the ballyhoo put out by Dalton Dray it was Annabel Brown. If you believe the ballyhoo put out by Bill Fontes it was Jeannie McFadden.

I remember people taking taxicab rides from bar to bar in Petaluma, and many of them stopped to see Annabel Brown and Jeannie McFadden.

Beside the Rose Court and the Villa Fontes there were other spots like the Colony Club — where marvelous entertainers from the past, who had faded from the limelight, were brought back and proved they still had a great deal of drawing power.

The Colony Club master of ceremonies was a colorful man named Fagan. At 2 o'clock in the morning he told the crowd, "You can't stay here, but you don't have to go home. There are other places." Many of them took his advice and went to hear Annabel Brown perform — the Rose Court being an "after hours" club. If you had the password, the person in charge at the door would let you in.

There were also top musical entertainers at the now gone Redwood Room of the Hotel Petaluma. Among those who entertained there were Earle Bond, who was known as the "Earl of Petaluma" and Kim Kimmell, who had an outstanding all-girl band.

That was a period when the ladies dressed in fancy clothing as they went to Petaluma's entertainment centers. It's interesting to note that many of the "Stage Door Johnnies" had ornate cigarette cases and silver flasks in which they carried their hard liquor. It's even more interesting to note that Jeannie McFadden and Annabel Brown didn't smoke or drink.

In those days bartenders dressed up in stylish clothing and sometimes in tuxedos.

With the changing times, the Rose Court after hours entertainment went back to closing at the legal hour of 2 o'clock in the morning. The Villa Fontes shut down and the "Stage Door Johnnies" vanished from the Petaluma scene — replaced by a more rowdy crowd. It was a man getting stabbed that brought down the final curtain on the Villa Fontes.

I don't know what became of McFadden or Brown. Bill Fontes died a good number of years ago and so did Dalton Dray. I've often wondered what became of the almost life-sized picture of Jeannie McFadden that hung on the wall of the Villa Fontes.

THE LIFE AND TIMES
OF THE COLORFUL C.P. PURCELL

When Clark Purcell died in 1986, it brought back many memories to a lot of Petalumans, and I was one of them. Known as C.P., Purcell was a colorful individual who had an unusual life.

During his high school days in Petaluma, C.P. was a brilliant student who preferred to be on the offbeat side of things. He went to several colleges, but never graduated from any. He once told me, "I just couldn't sit still long enough to make it through any of the higher institutions of education I attended."

During World War II he served in Burma, and after the war he became a globetrotter.

In numerous columns, I followed his activities and often referred to him as "Petaluma's Roaming Ambassador." He was also known as "Petaluma's Irish Rogue," a title he enjoyed and lived up to.

In years gone by he was the man who hosted those never-to-be-forgotten Finnigan's Balls on St. Patrick's Day in Petaluma.

The letters he mailed to the late Ray Wilson at his Petaluma Hideaway from all over the country were read by his local friends, who recognized him as a real Irish wit — a man with similar talents to Brendan Behan, the controversial and brilliant Irish author.

Those who remember C.P. and his Doberman pinscher, Hook, will tell you they were one of the most spectacular man and dog teams in the history of Northern California.

I remember the night a group of bullies who were scaring Russian River resort-goers bumped into C.P. Their terrorism came to an end when Hook jumped to his master's aid.

During his career as a globe-trotter, he helped build bridges in Washington, made the Alaskan scene, and worked on construction in almost every state.

There were times when C.P.'s closest friends didn't know where he was. When they were about to give him up as being lost forever, he would drift back to Petaluma, bringing the kind of excitement that made him one of Petaluma High School's all-time colorful students and alumni.

I traveled with C.P. on what could be called his shorter trips. One time we hopped a freight train, and after riding halfway to Santa Rosa, he jumped off. We toyed with the idea of turning hobo and riding freights around the country. I'm sorry we didn't.

He was 60 years old when the Grim Reaper took him, and I'm sorry to report he never wrote the book his friends hoped he would. I'm sure C.P. would have titled it something like: "The Adventures of a Wild Irish Rogue."

I like to refer to C.P. Purcell as a Petaluma product of the 1940s, the decade that changed the lives of millions of Americans. That was the decade that America became involved in World War II, and country boys who had never been more than 100 miles from home suddenly became world travelers. Unlike the boys who returned home and settled down, C.P. never stopped sowing his wild oats.

REUNITING WITH PHOTOJOURNALIST JOE ROSENTHAL

I recently attended a reunion that honored Joe Rosenthal, the man who took the picture of the flag being raised on Mount Sarabachi at Iwo Jima. The flag raising took place during World War II, and it is considered to be the greatest and most publicized war photo of all time.

In later years, I became a close friend of Joe's, and I'm proud to say that the first thing he did upon my arrival at the gathering in Novato was walk over and shake hands with me. After that we reminisced about our days at the now gone San Francisco Press Club. In those days Rosenthal was a top official at the Press Club. During his reign there I met many celebrated people, but the man who stood out as one of the foremost legends was Joe Rosenthal. In those days he knew all the people from small newspapers and they received the same treatment as those who worked for the gigantic publications.

Talking about Rosenthal, Ken Arnold, who was the official photographer for the San Francisco Press Club, said, "Rosenthal was the most sought-out person when celebrities and even legendary people visited the club. Most of them wanted their picture taken with him. Although his photo of raising the flag on Iwo Jima made him a world-wide celebrity, there is the Rosenthal that most people don't know."

Joe covered the San Francisco beat in one of the most exciting periods. He knew most of the colorful and world-shaking people that made San Francisco the most famous and interesting city to visit in the world.

One of Rosenthal's great virtues was that he put his love of people and love of country before making money.

Joe was more than a photographer. He was a first class journalist, and he gave me many stories that allowed me to scoop the larger newspapers. My time spent with him brought me a great deal of information about the news behind the headlines. He helped me with my slogan, "Columnist Soberanes has been photographed with more famous, infamous, usual and unusual people than anyone in the world. He's the world's number one people meeter." Joe not only gave me the opportunity to be photographed with them, he also made it a point to tell them I was a unique writer, who gave a straight story.

One of Rosenthal's great virtues was that he put his love of people and love of country before making money. Here's an example: He was offered large sums of money from advertising agencies to endorse their product by using his photo of the raising of the flag at Iwo Jima. He didn't talk much about the offers he received, but those at the reunion gathering said he could have become a multi-millionaire if he had accepted the offers. He did not.

At 90 years old, Rosenthal's sight is dimming, but not his memory. When he was called upon to speak, he gave a graphic description of Iwo Jima. He told how the military had underestimated the strength of the Japanese and how the military was wrong in figuring it would only take a few days and a few casualties to capture the island. Joe Rosenthal talked about the bloody battle of Iwo Jima and the thousands of both American and Japanese lives that were lost. He explained how the Japanese retreated to the many caves and how getting them out was a costly life and death struggle.

After the reunion with my friend Joe Rosenthal, I asked myself this question. "How many people would put American patriotism ahead of being a millionaire?" Joe Rosenthal is such a person.

MINGLING WITH
THE FAB FOUR

I met the Beatles during their first appearance in San Francisco and, after watching them and their fans perform for two days, I can truthfully say I've never seen anything like it.

A special platform was constructed at the San Francisco airport for the Beatles' arrival, and a heavy wire fence was set up around the platform. While thousands of wild-eyed teenagers (mostly girls from 12 to 15) milled around outside, I stood inside the fence with other members of the press, radio and television corps.

When the Beatles finally arrived, I was standing alongside two young reporters from London, England — N. Quenelle and Tim Street Porter. We checked the time, and according to our stopwatches, the Beatles were on this platform exactly 42 seconds. It could go down as the wildest 42 seconds in the history of San Francisco.

Girls — many of whom had stood in line for eight hours without food or water — were fainting. Other eager girls walked over their bodies as they tried to get closer to the wire fence where the press and Beatles were enclosed. Still others were in hysterics, and the police and ambulance crews were kept busy hauling those who had keeled over away from the scene.

One teenage girl, who had missed the Beatles, begged a policeman for his gun so she could kill herself. When the policeman refused, she tried to take the gun away from him.

Some of the girls were eating dirt, but it was special dirt because the Beatles had walked on it.

It was obvious to me that there wouldn't be any chance to contact the Beatles at the airport because they were immediately rushed away. I didn't know where they were going, so I made the following decision: Catch a bus to downtown San Francisco and catch another on to Petaluma. Well, the bus I was riding in stopped in front of the hotel where the Beatles were heading. I spotted Petaluman Ray Boccaleoni who was watching the activities. As the Beatles started up the stairs, I said, "Come on Ray, we are going up with them." He said, "They are heavily guarded and we won't be able to." My reply, "Watch my magic approach and we will."

A short time later we were in a locked room with the Beatles. Young people were trying to scale the walls of the hotel, and older guests were checking out of the hotel.

For the next few hours we remained locked in the hotel, and this gave me the opportunity not only to get acquainted with the Beatles, but to observe how they were hiding from their adoring fans and preparing for the concert. After the time in the hotel, Ray Boccaleoni went back to Petaluma and I attended the concert at the Cow Palace.

The excitement in the hotel room was mild compared to that at their concert. The concert started out with some other entertainers, but the crowd kept shouting, "We want the Beatles!"

When the Beatles appeared, thousands of young people screamed,

and here are some of the things that happened: Teenagers tried to rush the stage. One small girl knocked down a burly policeman who tried to restrain her. During the show, other teenagers passed out and some of them had to be forcibly held back by those in charge. I spotted one girl who had scratched her face with her fingernails and who was shouting, "I've never been so happy."

As the Beatles performed, hundreds of cameras flashed, and the auditorium lit up like a star-studded sky. The already energized crowd became more active, and the Beatles provided a spectacular show the likes of which I'd never seen before or since.

Although those attending the show were mostly teenagers, I remember the reporters from London saying, "We are predicting the Beatles will become the greatest musical group of the century."

I can now say they were right.

Jack Schallo, who said he was an old jazzman, turned to me and said, "The Beatles are among the greatest showmen and music makers I've ever heard."

People have asked me which of the Beatles talked the most while I was in the hotel with them? The answer is Ringo Starr. George Harrison was the quiet one.

I'll remember my contact with the Beatles as one of the most exciting of my career — a milestone. When I first met them there were four: now there are two. I was lucky enough to meet them when they were climbing the ladder that made them historic figures. Beatlemania spread worldwide and I'm sure it will be remembered for decades to come.

RIDING THE RAILS WITH SCISSORS SAM

The return of freight trains to Petaluma brought back memories of the hoboes who rode them. Today's story is about one of the best-known hoboes, Scissors Sam.

I last saw Scissors Sam, the legendary hobo, in June 1979. Since his appearance he added a number of marks of distinction to his already fabulous career as a "Knight of the Open Road".

In 1973, Sam won the title of "King of the Hoboes" in Britt, Iowa, where the hobo king is always crowned. During his last visit, he finished his third book, *Scissors Sam's Legendary Fireside Philosophy*. In it he tells the history of scissors, from almost the beginning of mankind to the present time. The book contains one of Sam's poems and much of his philosophy. He was proud of the fact that he was able to remember the addresses of thousands of people at whose homes he's stopped to sharpen scissors and spin yarns.

When he arrived in Petaluma in June 1979, he stopped at the home of Mrs. James Swan, who immediately put him to work sharpening scissors and tools. There he reminisced and looked to the future.

Scissors Sam is a man who likes to reminisce as well as keep up with the present and look towards the future. How did Scissors Sam become a hobo? "I started in 1927 when I ran away from my Pennsylvania home and the dirt farm where I was raised." In 1927 President Calvin Coolidge was finishing his first term, and Joseph Stalin was on the rise to power after Lenin's death.

"I was only 17, but the wanderlust had already taken control of me," Sam said. During the past 50 years he's had nothing to tie him down, and this is the way he wanted it.

One might think Scissors Sam would be a lonely man, but he points out, "I have thousands of satisfied customers in 48 states, and countless friends whose scissors I've sharpened. I probably visit more people than anyone in the country, so you can see why I'm not lonely."

PETALUMA MUSEUM ASSOCIATION

BILL SOBERANES WATCHES AS LIBERACE TRIES WRIST-WRESTLING

Scissors Sam is an expert on comparing the hobo, the tramp and the bum. The word "hobo", he says, was coined by a Catholic priest in 1865. The word came about because Civil War soldiers were finally free at the end of the war. Unlike today, these soldiers had to find their own way home and many became wanderers. Sam says the word hobo came from the Latin "homo bonus," which was interpreted as a freedom for man, or as a bonus that made men free after the Civil War. The Catholic priest, Sam said, took the first two letters from homo and bonus and combined them. Sam said a hobo is a free soul, a fellow who wants to see the world on his own terms. He has a desire to keep moving, and hasn't let society interfere with his life.

A tramp is a sea-going hobo who does the same thing on the sea as a hobo does on land. Sam said tramp sailors were responsible for the tramp steamers.

A bum, Sam said, is a person who won't work, is willing to live off others, and can be described as a person who lies around and does nothing.

Scissors Sam can remember when freight trains were loaded with hoboes, and railroad bulls would go as far as to throw them off a fast-moving train.

In 1976, Sam was flown first class on a jetliner to Washington, D.C., where he took part in a folk-like festival that featured unusual Americans. Sponsored by the Smithsonian Institution, its members helped record Sam's role in American folklore.

"Hoboes come from all walks of life," he said. "You find professors, doctors, and men like me who have decided being free is the only way to live. The hobo is the freest man in America."

He said hoboes have colorful names like Slow Norton, Just Plain Shorty, Prairie Slim. It's interesting to note Scissors Sam's real name is Calvin Long.

"Traveling and reading go hand in hand among many hoboes," Sam said. That's why he is able to converse on everything from the Bronze Age, when the scissors became an extremely useful tool, to what's going on today in political and scientific fields.

He claims to be the world's foremost expert on scissors. When I asked Scissors Sam what he would do if he suddenly became a millionaire, he said, "I'd do exactly what I've been doing for the past half century."

Yes, I believe in Santa Claus

All the people in my Fascinating World of People are real, not invented. The best-known person I've ever met is fictitious to some people, but very real to youngsters. His name is Santa Claus, and his role has been played by many wonderful individuals.

When Tomasini's Hardware was known as the North Pole of Petaluma, wonderful people like John Broxmeyer and Ole Olson became legendary Santa figures in Petaluma.

I remember "Two Ton" Tony Mazzolini, who ran the Yosemite Hotel, impersonating the jolly old gentleman by giving free food to those who arrived at his hotel on Christmas Eve and on Christmas Day. Santa has been pictured as a plump gentleman and the Two Ton Man really fit the bill in that department.

Petaluman Bill Symons characterized Santa as a musical personality for the older people he visited during the Christmas Season. He was also Santa for the Little Gnomes, Leprechauns and Chowder Marching Society during their Christmas marches. As Santa, Bill passed out goodies, sang Christmas songs, and played the harmonica.

One of Petaluma's really spectacular Santa Clauses was Earle Bond, whose music on the organ brought a lot of joy to Petalumans for many years. His Christmas tree was decorated with ornaments that people sent to him from all over the world.

Today we have a hitchhiking Santa Claus, who travels around gathering goodies for children. His name is Sparky Barger. Sparky has been hitchhiking as Santa for over 20 years, and by now he should be out on the road all over Northern California.

I took on the role of Santa Claus on several occasions myself — and on one of them I rode on a motorcycle with Petaluma policeman Al Bigelow. I even played Santa Claus at McKinley School. A young Pete Candage said, "You sound just like Bill Soberanes!"

The reaction to the strips was tremendous. I received mail from all over the world, with copies of the strips in numerous foreign languages. Many of those who wrote asked for information on Petaluma, and I had an incredible job trying to answer all the mail. Schulz's strips put Petaluma and wrist-wrestling on maps all over the world.

WRISTWRESTLING WITH SNOOPY

The news that Charles Schulz, creator of the cartoon strip, *Peanuts*, has retired because of illness got worldwide coverage in all branches of the media. My story about Schulz is personal and about his Petaluma connections.

I first met a young Schulz when I visited his home with Petaluman Paul Praetzel. My second encounter with him took place when he telephoned me and asked me if I thought he should put wrist-wrestling in his *Peanuts* cartoon. I said it was a great idea and to please do so. He asked me to send him information on the World's Wrist-Wrestling Championship that's held annually in Petaluma. Several months later he again telephoned me and said, "I am mailing you a present." The present turned out to be the complete original set of strips of Snoopy coming to Petaluma to wrist-wrestle.

The reaction to the strips was tremendous. I received mail from all over the world, with copies of the strips in numerous foreign languages. Many of those who wrote asked for information on Petaluma, and I had an incredible job trying to answer all the mail. Schulz's strips put Petaluma and wrist-wrestling on maps all over the world.

I later attended a gathering at the San Francisco Press Club honoring Schulz, and the topic of conversation was Snoopy and Petaluma. I posed for a wrist-wrestling photo with Schulz, and it later appeared in a number of newspapers.

During one of the tournaments, Schulz sent Snoopy to Petaluma as a mascot and the media gave Snoopy's appearance spectacular coverage. The news of his appearance made more headlines than the wrist-wrestling.

ELEVEN

Peanuts in Petaluma

In April and May of 1968, Charles M. Schulz introduced Petaluma to the world
in a series of his Peanuts comic strips – when Snoopy decided to compete in the
World Wrist-Wrestling Championships. Thanks to the good graces of
United Feature Syndicate, a selection of panels from that series is reproduced here.

TWELVE

Taking the Stage in Petaluma
by Janet Parmer

While Petaluma was burgeoning as a commercial and agricultural hub, opera singers, orators, actors, dancers, magicians, and even a talking horse were establishing the city as a performing arts mecca.

Lower Main Street, Petaluma, Cal.

THE UNIQUE THEATER IN THE BACKGROUND OF A VIEW OF MAIN STREET IN THE 1800S

SUNDAY MATINEE AT THE UNIQUE THEATER

While Petaluma was burgeoning as a commercial and agricultural hub, opera singers, orators, actors, dancers, magicians, and even a talking horse were establishing the city as a performing arts mecca. The Gem Theater, the American Theater, the Star Theater, the Kentucky Street Opera House, the Globe Theater, and the Unique Theater drew crowds from throughout the region. Coverage in Petaluma's newspapers illuminated what mattered to people during their leisure time – fireproof films, wholesome family entertainment, and low admission prices.

In an 1870 scrapbook entry, Mrs. L.P. Carpenter described the opening of an elegant opera house on Kentucky Street. "People came from hundreds of miles" to see shows, wrote Carpenter. The Washington Hall Association built the theater on the site of a livery stable. It was later known as the Petaluma Theater, and Finbar Devine's Irish pub now occupies the site.

A newspaper advertisement in 1899 for the Kentucky Street Opera House announced the drama "Uncle Tom's Cabin" as "the largest and best in the world featuring 20 colored and 20 white actors, plus bands, a cake walk, and a quartet of glockenspiel players."

In 1911, the Gem Theater in the Wickersham building on Main Street drew 800 people for the unveiling of its new player piano.

The Gem's owners described the place made of white marble and stucco as "strictly a first class theater." The Gem was one of several Petaluma theaters destroyed by fires.

An advertisement that same year for the American Theater on Main Street promoted it as "the favorite amusement resort of Petaluma. Highest grade of fireproof films used. Nothing objectionable put on. Ideal place to take the family evenings."

The following year, an ad for the Princess Theater, formerly the Star Theater, announced the opening of a play entitled "Alcohol."

The show, dedicated to the Women's Christian Temperance Union of America, was a "high class moral drama. Forty great scenes in the two-reel picture play."

Today, the cultural scene consists of theaters for live performances and movies, nightclubs with bands or disc jockeys supplying music, and an arts and lecture series at Santa Rosa Junior College. Nationally known authors speak at Copperfield's bookstore, music and dance schools showcase student accomplishments, and the Petaluma Historical Library and Museum sponsors many performing arts programs.

GEM THEATER FIRE, AUGUST 17, 1917

PHOENIX THEATER

Petaluma teenagers may take the Phoenix Theater for granted as an adolescent beacon on the corner of Washington and Keller streets, but the Phoenix has had a precarious existence for decades.

It was a sensation when it opened in 1904 as Hill Opera House, and was a huge draw on the vaudeville circuit. In later years, the theater struggled to survive. Idealistic and entrepreneurial owners gave it their best shot, experimenting with formats to appeal to the public's changing appetite for live theater, movies and music.

High school graduations, plays, wrist-wrestling competitions, poetry slams and memorial services have taken place in the cavernous space.

Under the sage and steady guidance of Tom Gaffey, its present manager, the Phoenix serves as a treasured hangout for many teens and a proving ground for musicians breaking into the professional performance scene. Many rock icons were given a chance to play on the Phoenix stage long before achieving stardom. "The way we've booked it forever is we get the one-offs, the larger stars play in a first market and in Petaluma on off nights," said Gaffey.

The Phoenix currently functions as more than a music venue. Kids come for homework help with peer tutors, adults spread out art supplies and encourage kids to paint wall murals, and a weekly health clinic provides a reliable place to get medical services. In addition, well-attended Alcoholics Anonymous and Narcotics Anonymous groups meet regularly, giving teenagers a safe, structured support system.

Caring, tuned-in adults, many of whom were once youthful Phoenix patrons, stop in for spontaneous chats.

"It's always survived. That's the point," said Gaffey, who worked at the theater as a teenager and returned in 1982 to manage it as an adult. "What people have done to keep it open in the last century is above and beyond economic sanity. There's always been somebody who wanted to keep it open."

Josephine Hill hired a San Francisco architect to design the Hill Opera House, which opened in 1904 with a production of Shakespeare's "Twelfth Night." *The Petaluma Argus* newspaper covered the dedication and gala:

"It was the most auspicious society gathering in the history of the city…It is a beautiful temple of music and drama…A dress affair with scores of beautiful costumes and beautiful women. The sound of pleasing music made a fairyland for all…. The grand opera house is ours to have and to hold and no wonder the breast of every Petaluman swells with pride when the opera house is mentioned."

The newspaper article concluded with this description: "It was almost midnight when delighted people rolled away from the elegant marble portals."

Peer inside the hulking gray and pink-trimmed Phoenix edifice today and one sees an entirely different scene. It's a dimly lit, unpretentious counter-culture space where teens flock to an indoor skateboard ramp, lounge on upholstered couches in the lobby, and practice ear-shattering music on stage.

ALIEN ANT FARM

HILL OPERA HOUSE

In its first incarnation, Hill Opera House was a wild success, and a 1911 newspaper story had the following headline: "Hill Opera House Figures in Monster Vaudeville Merger." The theater was responsible for putting Petaluma on the vaudeville map, bringing high-class acts to town. A newspaper advertisement described six big vaudeville acts and the promise "prices never change 10 cents, 15 cents, 25 cents." Among the varied acts on the Hill Opera House stage in its earliest years were the UC Glee Club, actress Lillie Langtry and Harry Houdini. World-renowned opera tenor Enrico Caruso sang there on his final trip to California in 1906.

In 1925, the opera house became part of the California Theater movie chain and Doc Naify later became manager. "He made everybody feel welcome. His legacy looms large here," said Gaffey.

In 1968, it was renamed the Showcase Theater, and in 1977, live music returned to the stage. Movie theater entrepreneur Dan Tocchini was one of the owners, and it changed hands several times before the Frankel family purchased it in 1981.

In 1986, Ken Frankel told a newspaper reporter he'd "lost money on everything" he attempted. Frankel started live concerts in addition to the movies, but was ready to convert to a primarily teen dance palace, responding to youth who'd collected hundreds of names on a petition urging the switch. "I've tried everything," said Frankel.

In 2001, the last time its survival was in jeopardy, a developer planned to purchase the site and tear down the aging building for new offices. Four high tech engineers, who became wealthy when Cerent was sold to Cisco Systems for $7 billion, stepped in at the last minute and offered to buy and restore the building. The men were music lovers, and a couple had played on the Phoenix stage or had children who were Phoenix regulars.

Paul Elliot, Chick Peterson, Keith Neuendorff and David Scott, aided by an impassioned plea from community leaders, triumphed in their quest — and two weeks before escrow closed, the developer agreed to pull out of the deal, allowing the foursome to buy it. Since the purchase in 2001 by the dot com engineers, the Phoenix has been run by the non-profit Petaluma Phoenix Center, Inc., and a board of directors.

"It's a real proving ground for new bands, but it's mainly a place for kids to socialize. A safe place to be off the streets and a place where they're allowed to be where people want them," said Jane Hamilton, executive director of the Phoenix Center.

CALIFORNIA THEATER FIRE, AUGUST 5, 1957

On one occasion, when three teenagers died, memorial services were held for them at the theater, and tributes were posted on the walls. "It's a place to express grief, rage, and love. It's for young people and major life transitions," she said.

The Phoenix name aptly describes the resurrection of the theater as a cultural and social gathering site for Petalumans despite disaster. Twice, fire damaged the building. In 1922, it was gutted by a blaze fueled by a neighboring paint store and was shut for one year for repairs. In 1957, when it was known as the California Theater, fire swept through again, destroying the roof. But like the mythical phoenix, after a six-month closure for repairs, it rose again and reopened.

In 1979, it became the Phoenix Theater, and a few years later Gaffey agreed to manage the place. "I thought I'd take the job for a year. It was pandemonium loaded with kids. They told me, 'We run the place.' It was a hoot and a holler. The game was on and my buddies and I ran it," said Gaffey. Under Gaffey's management, many rising bands performed, including Santana, Red Hot Chili Peppers, Green Day, Primus, Jimmy Cliff, Metallica and Alien Ant Farm. "We were a premier punk house, no doubt about it. We gradually evolved and for years operated with no money," said Gaffey. He sees the Phoenix as a "people's" theater. "I feel the best karma is to let it be used," he said. "It loves it when it's used. The building has it own soul."

MYSTIC THEATER

When word spread that Irish singer/songwriter Van Morrison would play the Mystic Theater in downtown Petaluma, the show sold out in 27 minutes. Morrison hadn't played a concert in the United States for four years, and it was a significant coup for the Mystic when Morrison's promoter phoned in 1992 requesting to book him. Mystic owner Jeff Harriman and manager Ken O'Donnell invested thousands of dollars to upgrade the acoustics and electricity to the standards a rock icon like Morrison would expect, but it was well worth it. The improvements – and the notoriety gained by hosting Morrison — propelled the Mystic into the major league of Bay Area rock concert venues.

Morrison's on-stage demeanor surprised and elated his loyal fans. "He came here to kick off his tour because he wanted to be somewhere obscure," said O'Donnell. "He played directly to the audience for four hours straight. He usually turns his back to the crowd."

O'Donnell ranks that concert, and another Mystic show featuring the Blind Boys of Alabama — and the Spirit of the Century Band with Charlie Musselwhite, John Hammond, and David Lindley — as "spiritual experiences, the best two shows hands down I've ever seen in my life." Although he can hear live music most nights of the week at the Mystic, he postponed a vacation to Costa Rica to attend the Blind Boys and Spirit of the Century concert.

Managing a medium-sized concert hall in a medium-sized city is not for the faint of heart. It takes an enduring passion for music — and unswerving faith in music promoters and musicians — to book shows expecting audiences will buy tickets, appreciate the music, and continue patronizing the theater.

VAN MORRISON

CHARLIE MUSSELWHITE

The Mystic, which opened as a vaudeville venue in 1911, has impeccable acoustics and a charming, intimate ambiance with seating for 550 people. Business tycoon John A. McNear built the original Mystic Theater, putting a talking horse on stage as the first act when the theater opened. His son, John A. McNear, Jr., later owned the theater.

Vaudeville groups, dancers, ventriloquists and comedians entertained Petalumans at the Mystic. In the late 1920s, the Mystic's name changed to the State Theater, and in the 1930s it was closed temporarily to install costly electrical wiring for movies with sound, known as "talkies". It originally had an orchestra pit, which was later removed. By the 1940s, it was primarily a movie house with an occasional concert. Local movie theater entrepreneur Dan Tocchini owned the theater; he sold it to Al Finley in the 1970s and, at that point, it began showing pornographic movies.

When Jeff Harriman purchased the two-story mixed use building in 1976, he boarded it up and did a massive remodeling, removing a furniture store and motorcycle shop located in commercial space on the first floor and renovating offices upstairs. Following the building upgrade, an adjacent restaurant, known as the Petaluma Café, was rented out. In 1978, Ben Myron and Don Taylor operated the Palace Theater, showing classics, foreign movies and new releases.

In 1987, Harriman took over the restaurant, renaming it McNear's Saloon and Dining House. Ken O'Donnell joined him in 1988 and, two years later, they took ownership of the movie theater. Under their management, the restaurant began hosting live music in its upstairs room. When a 1991 show featuring the Arc Angels and Doyle Bramhall III sold out the Mystic, the pair decided to try booking more national touring acts into the theater.

After the pivotal Van Morrison gig, the Mystic began attracting well-known touring acts such as Leon Russell and Taj Mahal. The band, Train, which has since become a popular national act, played the Mystic 10 times before it achieved rock stardom. As a teenager and young adult, O'Donnell frequented the Fillmore and Great American Music Hall in San Francisco, and he now tries to emulate their successful formula of booking an eclectic talent mix — a blues artist with a rocker or a surf guitarist like Dick Dale with drummer and singer Buddy Miles.

"I started out picking artists that would sell out the venue. Half the people who play come back because they want to play here," said O'Donnell.

Vaudeville groups, dancers, ventriloquists and comedians entertained Petalumans at the Mystic. In the late 1920s, the Mystic's name changed to the State Theater, and in the 1930s it was closed temporarily to install costly electrical wiring for movies with sound, known as "talkies."

CARLOS SANTANA

JOHN HIATT

Among the well-known musicians who've performed at the Mystic are Carlos Santana, John Hiatt, Hot Tuna, Yonder Mountain String Band, Leo Kottke, Iris Dement, Ben Harper, Waylon Jennings, Michael Franti, Bela Fleck, Robert Earl Keen and Mose Allison.

It's a challenge to attract audiences to performances by unfamiliar bands, however, even if tickets are moderately priced. "The hardest thing is they don't come out for new acts," O'Donnell says. "The Petaluma demographic is they don't go out to see people they don't know." He's committed to showcasing new, young bands, but needs to fill the theater at least halfway to break even. "We try to help local bands, but we sometimes get killed trying to do it…but we keep trying anyway even if they play as openers for larger acts."

O'Donnell, who is assisted with bookings by Sheila Groves of Notable Talent, is aware of the importance of bringing in acts that appeal to young audiences. A recent show by Pepper sold out in minutes. Slightly Stoopid also sold out rapidly when word that it was coming to town spread among its teenage and twenty-something disciples.

CINNABAR THEATER

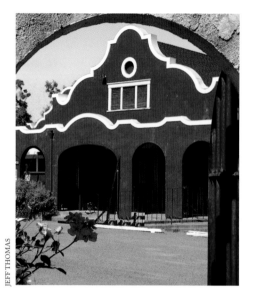

MARVIN AND JAN KLEBE
PHOTO FROM JAN'S
PERSONAL COLLECTION

JEFF THOMAS

What started as a visionary's dream to provide an artistic home for actors, singers and dancers has become an ingrained part of Petaluma's cultural life. The Cinnabar Theater, a Mission Revival style building on the northern rural outskirts of town, is a creative incubator for professional artists.

Although the rural, cinnabar-colored building with fanciful white trim may look like the home of a community theater, the choices made by the Cinnabar Theater's creative directors have established the theater as a maverick — a place where risks are taken and audiences regularly experience high quality cutting edge theater, opera, and dance. Performers working in major theaters readily make the trek to Petaluma to appear in Cinnabar shows, which draw audiences from throughout the Bay Area.

The odd theater tucked behind the trees on a knoll was known for its hippies on the hillside, but that didn't faze Marvin and Jan Klebe. Marvin Klebe, a baritone who had performed in Europe and

with the San Francisco Opera, was eager to nurture his own theater program. He'd become disillusioned with the professional opera world because it was too structured, lacked innovation, and wasn't conducive to raising a family. The Klebes evaluated buildings in the area for their ambitious live/work space, with Marvin testing acoustics by singing in available schools, churches, and grange halls — looking for a place to fulfill his vision. The shell of a former two-room schoolhouse seemed promising, and Klebe figured he could set up a wood shop and support his family as a cabinetmaker while pursuing his artistic dream. The Klebes purchased the circa-1908 former school from the fraternal order of Eagles in 1970 and moved their family of four young sons into the dilapidated structure. This would become their unorthodox home — and a place where thousands of artists would find a creative "home."

Aloysha Klebe, who serves as Cinnabar's facilities director and manages the expanded wood shop on the premises, remembers what it was like as a nine-year-old boy to move from a conventional house into the former school building. "This is cool. This is different. We lived in the front room, which is now the theater."

Elly Lichenstein, Cinnabar Theater's executive director, recalls that "Marvin was sick and tired (of the opera scene) and needed to feel more responsible to himself as an artist. Jan told him to stop complaining and make something happen. He thought he would make a livelihood here, and poured money into this place until the day he died. Well, he thought so at the beginning, but it became apparent to him right away that this was a pipe dream."

Klebe, who passed away in 1999, was a gifted singer and director, and his charismatic leadership attracted colleagues who continue an open-ended quest to cultivate creativity and stage productions, including some experimental ventures.

During the last few decades, the Klebe family, with the help of community volunteers, has gradually restored and expanded the stucco structure. In 2007, a massive work crew from Rebuilding Together pitched in by replacing a floor, windows, renovating the antiquated dressing rooms, and making other essential building improvements.

"All sorts of people have come through and made a footprint on it," says Aloysha Klebe.

Cinnabar's first production in 1972 was "The Bicycle," which Lichenstein described as "some weird opera." Since then, the Cinnabar has staged many operas that may be unfamiliar to audiences — but stretch their artistic sensibilities with top-notch performances. Cinnabar also stages plays that are not commonly performed and contracts with playwrights to create new productions that can premiere in Petaluma.

MARVIN KLEBE AND CAST IN MR. KLEBE'S SIGNATURE ROLE, *THE MAN OF LA MANCHA*

ELLY LICHENSTEIN AND MARVIN KLEBE IN *BLUEBEARD'S CASTLE*, 1990

COURTESY CINNABAR THEATER

CLOCKWISE FROM TOP LEFT: 1. BHARATI SOMAN AS COUNTESS ROSINA IN *THE MARRIAGE OF FIGARO* 2. LEFT TO RIGHT: CLAIRE VICTOR, ELLY LICHENSTEIN AND MARVIN KLEBE IN "COLE: PORTER'S PEOPLE", 1994 3. KEVIN COURTEMANCHE AS CANIO, ERINA NEWKIRK AS NEDDA AND WILLIAM NEELY AS TONIO IN *PAGLIACCI* 4. DANIELLE LEVIN AS PEGEEN AND BRODERICK VALENTINE AS CHRISTY IN *PLAYBOY OF THE WESTERN WORLD*

STEVEN YEAGER

JEFF THOMAS

JEFF THOMAS

The original resident companies included choreographer and dancer Ann Woodhead's Mercury Moving Company, Klebe's Cinnabar Opera Theater, and director Richard Blake's Quicksilver Theater Company. In the early days, performers were frequently unpaid. Now, they earn a respectable income, similar to that paid by other professional theater companies. "The vision is that we know the best art comes from respect for the artist," says Lichenstein. "It can't be corporate and can't be dictated. It's the artist who makes the minute decisions."

With financial support from various sources, including contributions from city revenues, Cinnabar organized an elaborate, three-week Music Festival every summer for 15 years, bringing world music, classical and chamber pieces, candlelight concerts, and shows for kids. Music director Nina Shuman helped locate music selections and performers not frequently heard in Sonoma County – again stretching cultural boundaries for local audiences and musicians. The Music Festival has been on hiatus, but Cinnabar hopes to resurrect it as funding becomes available.

A milestone for Cinnabar came in 1983 when the theater was asked to create an after-school program for the nearby Cinnabar School. "It was a huge turning point for us," says Lichenstein.

EMILY BROWN AND KYLE GEE IN THE 2005-06 CINNABAR YOUNG REP PRODUCTION OF *ORPHEUS IN THE UNDERWORLD*

"Kids were working with professionals, and we said 'Oh, this is something we need to do.'" Thus, Cinnabar's Young Repertory Theater was launched. It is now a year-round entity with classes, workshops, summer camps and productions featuring children and teenagers.

Young Rep also started a program to bring students to the theater for operas, and commissioned new operas for kids, but it was halted due to funding cuts.

Young Repertory Theater activities now represent half of the Cinnabar's programs, and an annual chili cook-off attracting amateur and professional chefs raises money to help defray the costs of running the classes, staging the kids' productions, and making scholarships available.

Although the youth program struggles to be self-sustaining, the theater's board and administrative staff are committed to the cause. As Lichenstein explains, former students who are working in the theatrical world, as well as in other professions, have credited their Cinnabar training as a crucial part of their personal and cultural development. "They come back to Cinnabar and say this is where I developed myself as a human being."

DANIELLE CAIN AS ROSE AND TIM KNIFFIN AS ANTONY IN *ENCHANTED APRIL*

KIRA DILLS-DESURRA AND CAST FROM THE 2004-05 YOUNG REP PRODUCTION OF *THE TAILOR OF GLOUCESTER*

THIRTEEN

SESQUICENTENNIAL STUDENT ART

IN THE SPRING OF 2007, THE PETALUMA ARTS ASSOCIATION PARTNERED WITH THE PETALUMA SESQUICENTENNIAL COMMITTEE TO SPONSOR AN ART CONTEST FOR 7TH THROUGH 12TH GRADE STUDENTS. THE THEME WAS "PETALUMA'S PAST, PRESENT & FUTURE." WINNING ENTRIES WERE EXHIBITED AT ART IN THE PARK THAT SEPTEMBER. SEVERAL OF THE IMAGES WERE CHOSEN TO ILLUSTRATE CHAPTERS OF THIS BOOK, BUT ALL WERE IMPRESSIVE — SO WE DECIDED TO SHOW THE REST OF THEM HERE.

MIRANDA ASHE

JAMAINE O'CONNELL

TARA FUNK

KATE HORICK

JUSTIN ISAACSON

AUSTIN JAY

MICAELA MADDEN

MONIKA BREITHAUPT

KASEY ENGLAND

RYAN STAGE

VALERIE RUSTAD

LAUREN HEALD

HALEY KEEGAN

KAITLIN LUCCHESI

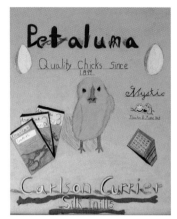

ANDY SCHARF

KATE ARNTZ

KELSIE GUGEL

RACHEL FINER

MARK TOMASEK

JUSTIN RINGLEIN

VANESSA ROMERO

NICK JENSEN

DOMINIQUE MAGLIULO

STEPHANIE MOORE

SHANE KINAHAN

ALYSE WITTE

LAURA PUGH

FOURTEEN

HOW THE THEATRE DISTRICT GOT ITS THEATRE

In the summer of 2007, Theatre Square opened. It was the final piece in the biggest development project in downtown Petaluma's history.

In the summer of 2007,

Theatre Square opened. It was the final piece in the biggest development project in downtown Petaluma's history. In fact, no multi-building addition had been made to the Historic Downtown area since John A. McNear built another theater — still just a block away on Petaluma Boulevard North — in 1911.

Theatre Square is part of a project covering nearly four square blocks — between B and D Streets on the north and south and First Street and Petaluma Boulevard on the east and west. Included are more than a hundred residential lofts and apartments, dozens of retail and restaurant spaces, multiple office suites, a parking structure, and a riverfront park and promenade. The centerpiece, of course, is a twelve-screen complex of motion picture theaters, giving the development its name: the Theatre District.

Architecturally, the Theatre District takes it cues from the historic buildings it adjoins — brick and metal-clad warehouses and century-old facades. Conceptually, though, the development reflects thoroughly modern ideas. It's a high-density complex of mixed use spaces. As developer Basin Street Properties describes it in their advertising, "Live Here. Work Here. Play Here."

Anchoring the plaza in Theatre Square is a tiled fountain encrusted with handmade ceramic faces. These "Faces of Petaluma" were created by Petaluma citizens — mostly children — at a community event sponsored by Basin Street Properties and the Petaluma Area Chamber of Commerce's Leadership Petaluma class of 2005.

For a dozen years, the Leadership Petaluma program has sought to build strong leaders from all sectors of our community — businesses, public service and nonprofit organizations, education, and citizens-at-large. Participants make a ten-month commitment to explore Petaluma's history, commerce, demographics, public service, labor, and overall culture. In addition, Leadership classmates form lasting personal and professional relationships through team-building exercises that culminate in planning and implementing community service projects.

Besides the "Faces of Petaluma" fountain, Leadership Petaluma classes have been involved in creating the Heritage Wall mural at the corner of Washington Street and Petaluma Boulevard and the Labyrinth at Oak Hill Park, renovation work at Polly Hannah Klaas Performing Arts Center and the San Antonio Day Care Center playground, planning a community garden with PEP Housing, creating a garden at Bernard Eldridge Elementary School, and many other valuable community projects.

The most impressive contribution to the Theatre District, however, was not one that was made by adult community leaders. Instead, it was the result of four years of concerted effort by seven girls who were just twelve years old when they decided Petaluma needed a movie theater. Even more than the burgeoning growth downtown, the ability and drive of these young women bodes well for Petaluma's future.

The following is their story, told in their own words.

— TERRY SMITH, WITH ASSISTANCE
FROM KAREN LUTTRELL-LANGDON

HOW THE THEATRE DISTRICT GOT ITS THEATRE

BY TAYLOR NORMAN, ASHLEY DITMER, LIZA HALL, LIZ COMSTOCK, SARAH MARCIA, NOELLE BISSON AND MADISON WEBB—"THE SUPERB SEVEN"—AND PATTY NORMAN

JUST BEFORE STARTING THEIR PROJECT IN SEVENTH GRADE — LEFT TO RIGHT, STANDING: LIZA HALL, LIZ COMSTOCK, SARAH MARCIA, MADISON WEBB, TAYLOR NORMAN; LYING IN FRONT: NOELLE BISSON, ASHLEY DITMER

TERRY SMITH COURTESY *THE PETALUMA POST*

TERRY SMITH COURTESY *THE PETALUMA POST*

In November of 2001, a group of us were walking home from Petaluma Junior High, where we were all in 7th grade. We wanted to go to the movies that evening, and we were debating which, if any, of our moms might be willing to drive us to the movie theaters in Rohnert Park. We were gloomily predicting that no one would. Although none of us remembers who actually said the words, by the time we'd gotten to Ashley's house, we'd decided we should open our own theaters in Petaluma, "since the grown-ups will never do it."

Taylor's mom arrived to pick up Taylor and heard our conversation. She liked our spirit and challenged us to pursue our goal. We jumped at the chance, and she told us if we were willing to work hard and commit to our goal, we could meet every week at Taylor's house and she'd give us whatever guidance we needed. The next Wednesday was the first meeting — and by then we'd already christened our theaters "the Superb Seven Cinemas" — taken from the name our parents had for our group.

At our first meeting, we realized how much we didn't know, and we began coming up with tasks.

SARAH: Develop a list of 10-15 of the most major Bay Area celebrities, particularly movie stars.

TAYLOR: Develop a list of all the movie theaters in Sonoma County and Novato — including number of screens, admission price, days and hours open, and distance from Petaluma.

LIZA: Find all the articles in the *Press Democrat* over the last year that have to do with the movie theater situation in Petaluma. Check the *Argus*, too.

MADISON: Develop a list of the 10 wealthiest people in the Bay Area and the 10 wealthiest people in Sonoma County.

NOELLE: Develop a list of the 10 largest, most profitable companies in the Bay Area and the 10 largest, most profitable companies in Sonoma County.

LIZZY: Develop a list of expenses for equipment necessary for food service at a movie theater. Find out what can be leased, what must be purchased. Look on eBay to see if there is any used equipment available.

ASHLEY: Develop a packet of the material you've already researched, plus any more you can find, on starting a movie theater — including a list of helpful web sites and a list of books that might be useful.

After we regrouped the following Wednesday — with research in hand — we realized we were serious, and Taylor's mom took us more seriously, as well.

After that, we brainstormed at every meeting. Who did we know? Who could help us learn more? We asked our parents and our parents' friends.

One of the first places to lend us a hand was the tiny little Rio Theater in Monte Rio — an independent, single screen movie house right next to the Russian River. Someone knew the owners, and an information meeting and tour was set up. Don and Suzy, the owners of the Rio, spent nearly two hours with us, teaching us everything from what it's like to own a theater — "Your most important tools are a broom and a dustpan" — to how movies are booked, what they cost, and how to thread reels of film onto a projector. We came away enthused by our visit and undaunted by the enormity of our project.

Our next project was determining what things cost and how we could make money for a project no one else seemed to want to take on. We scheduled a meeting with the VP of Finance from a large theater chain to learn as much as we could and spent a Wednesday night eating our way through a complimentary case of Skittles and taking notes on the various ways theaters make money.

By early February, we had begun researching and writing our business plan. Each of us contributed a section, and that became the section she would speak on when we made presentations. Early meetings with members of the City Council, Planning Commission, and business leaders provided us with a great deal of information, experience and confidence.

In April, the *Argus-Courier* ran a story on us, and we still remember one of us saying, "We're really going to do this!"

We realized we needed to finish the financial piece of our business plan. We spent several meetings estimating attendance month by month at a seven-screen theater, estimating ticket prices, and estimating concession income. This led to our first meeting with Matt White and Scott Stranzl of Basin Street Properties, who helped us figure out the costs of building, construction and parking. All of our estimates and data were loaded into an Excel spreadsheet, and Taylor's mom typed and instructed us on basic accounting facts. The result was impressive, and later, when we met with David Shesgreen, the president of the Century Theater chain, he was knocked out by the accuracy of our projections and estimates.

We also began attending more meetings: the Downtown Central Specific plan, City Council meetings and others. We realized that parking was a big issue, and we began looking for space that might become available. We also attended several film festivals and toured behind the scenes at other theater chains, learning how multi-screen theaters were run. We were completely possessed by our movie theater dream.

As our plan came together in the summer of 2002, we realized the biggest hurdle we faced was coming up with financing. We reviewed the list of local celebrities and big businesses we'd compiled and kept coming back to one name: George Lucas. We felt he had the resources, the spirit and the local connection to be a source for us, so we set our goal on getting an opportunity to meet with him. We presented our plan to one local Lucasfilm employee, who put us in touch with another — and eventually presented our plan to Tim Schafbuch, the head of THX. He was delighted by our presentation and offered to deliver a letter from us to George Lucas:

Dear Mr. Lucas,

We are a group of seven 13-year-old girls living in Petaluma, California. Our town — with a population of over 50,000 — hasn't had a movie theater for the last year and a half, and we are tired of waiting for the adults to do something about it. We have decided to figure out a way to open our own theater.

We have written a business plan and presented it to many Petaluma officials. We have learned a great deal, and we know that although our goal will be difficult to reach, it will be worth all of our hard work if we are successful.

We know that you are very busy, but we would like to request the opportunity to present our plan to you. Please don't misunderstand — we aren't looking for you to fund our plan. However, if we had input from you, and people knew you had encouraged us, it might open more doors. We believe our plan is well thought out and unique, and that you would find our ideas interesting. Besides, we think it is ironic that you made your first commercially successful movie, "American Graffiti," in our town, and now we don't even have a movie theater.

Please let us know if you have the time to meet with us. We'll brighten your day!

Thank you, Superb Seven

A little over two weeks later, we got a message asking us to call Jeanne Cole at Lucasfilm. George Lucas had invited us to meet with the president, vice president and two directors. A meeting was set up, and we began practicing our presentation skills. Two nights before we were scheduled to go to Lucasfilm, we had a dress rehearsal in Taylor's front room. Many of our initial contacts were invited to attend, along with favorite teachers. The next day was spent fine-tuning, making poster boards, name cards, copies of business plans for each of the Lucas executives. The following day, we drove to Skywalker Ranch. Each of us had a worry stone — something Taylor's mom had given us for luck (and to keep us from fidgeting).

Lucasfilm's Public Relations Director, Jeanne Cole, describes the meeting:

"Not long ago George Lucas received a letter from a group of seven junior high school girls (they refer to themselves as the Superb Seven) from the town of Petaluma in Sonoma County. The girls are determined to get a movie theater opened in Petaluma. Instead of waiting for adults to do something about it, they have taken matters into their own hands. The town of 55,000 has not had a movie theater since Pacific Theaters closed their doors in March, 2001.

"They now wanted to present their plan to Lucasfilm. As a courtesy I scheduled a meeting … with [Lucasfilm President] Gordon Radley, Jim Ward, VP of Marketing, Lynne Hale, Director of Communications and myself. Quite honestly, I looked forward to the meeting as a diversion from the day-to-day business of *Star Wars* — something new, something different and at the very least an excuse to schedule an afternoon meeting where cookies and milk would be served! As a resident of Petaluma, I have also been missing having a movie theater in town but hadn't done anything about it except grumble.

"They began their presentation and from that moment we were all captivated. I have been with Lucasfilm for eleven years and have had to sit through many presentations from potential promotional partners to studio executives and I have never seen a group present in such a clear, concise and articulate manner. These girls were prepared, confident, and poised. We were all impressed with the quality and sophistication of their presentation. We had assumed the meeting would be a "meet and greet" and last about thirty minutes. They had our full attention and our interest for almost two hours. (Remember, these girls are in 7th grade and are twelve years old.) When they finished presenting they asked for questions and comments. We thought at first that perhaps they were just well rehearsed, but when we began quizzing them we knew immediately that these girls really knew their stuff.

"At the end of the meeting we suggested to the girls that they should come up with an event that would build community support and media interest in their cause. Ten days later they sent an e-mail describing their plan for a Petaluma rally. After meeting with local civic leaders and teen groups the girls gathered additional support and attained all the proper permits and permissions to hold a rally next week. On October 23rd at 7 p.m. the Superb Seven will present an outdoor, digitally-projected screening of 'American Graffiti' (filmed in Petaluma by George Lucas in 1973) on Petaluma Boulevard on the wall of the old Victory Chevrolet building. The rally is free. All you need to bring is a beach chair, a blanket to keep you warm and it's BYOP (bring your own popcorn). The Petaluma firefighters have volunteered to do security in exchange for a couple of days of the girls rolling fire hoses. Teachers have been asked to give extra credit or a homework pass for attending this civic event.

"The girls have even come up with a slogan, 'Coming Soon — A Theater Near You'. And you know what? I think they're right. If anybody can do it, these girls can. They are amazing and I think there is a good story here. It's a story of young women finding their power and using it and not giving up no matter how daunting the task, it's about city politics, land development issues and the exhibition side of the movie industry."

During the meeting at Lucasfilm, one of us asked Gordon Radley if we could call him if we had any questions. He took off his glasses, looked seriously at all of us, and said "Girls, we will not leave you in this project. We're with you all the way." He wasn't kidding.

The "American Graffiti" event was an unqualified success. We received great coverage live on ABC channel 7 and an article in the *San Francisco Chronicle*. Gordon Radley arranged for us to meet with Century theaters and present our plan to Century president David Shesgreen. Although we couldn't entice Century to open a theater in Petaluma, we kept at it.

We appeared at countless Planning Commission and City Council meetings, repeating our message — a downtown theater complex that everyone could get to easily. A last-minute arrangement between Basin Street Properties and the City of Petaluma created an opportunity we'd always believed was possible — a theater complex in downtown Petaluma on the very site where we'd shown "American Graffiti".

In June of 2004, we invited Lucasfilm president Gordon Radley to lunch. We wanted to update him on the theater plans, show him the blueprints that Basin Street had provided us with, and ask his advice on some ideas. He was delighted to accept, and was undeterred when he realized we didn't get out of school until 3 p.m. — a bit late for lunch. Instead, he drove to Petaluma and met us at Quinleys, where we all had curly fries and milk shakes and sat around a table in the park with the drawings. A representative from Basin Street Properties joined us and we walked around the proposed theater site.

LEFT: GRAND OPENING OF THE BOULEVARD CINEMAS, WITH THEIR STARS — LEFT TO RIGHT: LIZ COMSTOCK, ASHLEY DITMER, LIZA HALL, PATTY NORMAN (MENTOR), TAYLOR NORMAN, SARAH MARCIA, MADISON WEBB, NOELLE BISSON

RIGHT: AS GRAND MARSHALS OF THE 2005 BUTTER & EGG DAYS PARADE — LEFT TO RIGHT, ASHLEY DITMER, MADISON WEBB, LIZ COMSTOCK, TAYLOR NORMAN, SARAH MARCIA; IN FRONT OF CAR: NOELLE BISSON, LIZA HALL

In January of 2005, we all attended the groundbreaking ceremonies for the new theater, and we all got to turn the earth with the ceremonial shovels. In April, 2005, we were honored to be asked to be the Grand Marshals of the Butter & Egg Days parade. We'd all been going to the parade as spectators, or marching in it with Brownies and Girl Scouts, for most of our lives. We'd never dreamed of being the Grand Marshals.

On May 17, 2005, the theaters opened with a great deal of fanfare. We were interviewed by every Bay Area news station. The Northern California Classic Car Club provided each of us with a beautiful, *American Graffiti*-era car in which to ride to the opening ceremony. When we got there, flashbulbs popped, and video cameras hovered as we were interviewed. We knew we weren't really famous, but it was fun to pretend. Seeing our names in gold stars permanently embedded in the sidewalk in front of the theaters was a tremendous thrill.

Since then, we've continued to be involved with the theaters. All of us have worked at the theater except for Madison, who moved to Sacramento our freshman year. We were interviewed for the *Today Show* in August, 2005. That same summer, we had the heady experience of having a Los Angeles-based film production company option the rights to our story. In September of 2006, we were invited to be the keynote speakers at the California Downtown Association's annual convention in Monterey, a

KELLY KEHOE

gathering of mayors from small towns all over California. They gave us (and our town) a standing ovation when we finished.

Gordon Radley has kept in touch, as he vowed he would. He advised us when filmmakers optioned the rights to our story, attending negotiation dinners and reviewing legal documents. He wrote letters of recommendation for our college applications, and most recently, he attended our high school graduation from Petaluma High — standing patiently in the heat to hear each of our names called.

We all have remained friends, and are now off to new adventures in college and beyond. Ashley is going to Clark University in Massachusetts, Liz will be at Arizona State University, Taylor will be at UC Berkeley, Noelle will be at UC Santa Cruz, Madison will be at UC San Diego, Liza will be at Cal Poly, and Sarah will be at CSU Monterey Bay.

Were we disappointed to not actually own the theaters? Honestly, at the time? Yes. Now, though, we know how much we didn't know.

We learned a lot, and earned a great deal of respect from the Petaluma community. Not many 12-year-olds would have taken on such a task, or stayed with it for four years — but quite possibly, not many cities would've made such an effort to listen. We learned what power individuals have, and that lesson will take us far. It's been said that Petaluma was lucky to have us. We believe we were lucky to grow up in Petaluma.

SCOTT HESS

"No matter what obstacles we faced, we plowed through them as long as we kept sight of what was ultimately important in the end."

TAYLOR NORMAN

"This is the biggest concept we have learned thus far: to realize that we can make a difference in this world."

ASHLEY DITMER

"When seven pre-teens can start with an idea and turn it into a reality through five years of growing, loving, learning and even a little fighting, you learn that nothing can stop you if you are really determined."

LIZ COMSTOCK

"Throughout my experience as a member of the Superb Seven, I cherished the friendships. We have all known each other since elementary school, some even longer, and we still get along and have fun."

LIZA HALL

"Now that it's all over, I take on challenges with a new perspective. If you make your work fun and truly believe in your cause, it won't seem like work at all."

SARAH MARCIA

"When I try to imagine what I would be like if we never felt the initiative to go for the unimaginable, I see a young naïve girl who never would have realized she had the power to achieve her dreams."

NOELLE BISSON

"Overall the experience really empowered me, and gave me not only greater confidence, but the knowledge that success is never out of reach."

MADISON WEBB

FIFTEEN

FAMOUS WINES & VIBRANT VINES OF THE PETALUMA GAP
by Von Hurson

Crest a hill, round a curve, look into the little nooks and crannies that make up the Lakeville, Adobe Road, or west county landscape, and you'll notice more and more pockets of green, made up of rows and rows of grape vines.

VINEYARD IN FOG

LANCE KUEHNE

They're tucked and hidden in the most unexpected places. Crest a hill, round a curve, look into the little nooks and crannies that make up the Lakeville,

Adobe Road, or west county landscape, and you'll notice more and more pockets of green, made up of rows and rows of grape vines. The vines bring brilliant patches of color to the golden grasses that support the neighboring pastures of cows and sheep. They're so idyllic, so pastoral, and so beautiful. These are the vines of the Petaluma Gap and the source of some of the most exciting wines to hit the California wine scene in a very long time. "Petaluma Gap" is a quirky name for a wine growing region, isn't it? You'd think they could have picked something more romantic or esoteric. But that's not what this area is, and that's not who these people are. Quite frankly, there is nothing that more accurately describes this area as well as "The Gap." It gives the wines produced here a certain panache — a *Nom de Guerre* that is catchy, totally descriptive and as unforgettable as the wines themselves.

The wines we're talking about come from vines that have been planted in the last ten to twenty years. However, it's what happened long ago that provides the backdrop and impetus for today's Petaluma Gap. Because of the river, the California Gold Rush had more of an influence here than elsewhere and where there were high-spirited miners, there had to be wine. Men of vision saw a bright future in grape growing and, as they say, "The rest is history."

DAYS OF OLD

In the mid-1800s, vineyards were prevalent throughout rural Petaluma. The thriving Victorian riverfront city served as a watering hole, as well as a shipping channel to transport mining supplies, grains and other food products for the miners heading to the hills in search of gold. Situated on a waterway that provided year-round transportation to San Francisco, Petaluma was a natural location for producing and shipping wine, and wines traveled from warehouses in the downtown district of Petaluma, along the river, to San Francisco and beyond. Vineyards sprang up within the Petaluma Gap area, producing wines for both the locals and the hordes of "'49ers" that were flocking to San Francisco and the Sierras.

In 1989, author William F. Heintz completed a fascinating historical document at the behest of the Sangiacomo family, of Sangiacomo vineyard fame. The extensive study records the history of wines and viticulture in the Lakeville area from its earliest beginnings, and much of the information that follows is summarized from that document.

There is an excitement in unearthing the names of the grape growers and wine makers of a bygone day. The early wine pioneers might not be as well-known as those who founded the more famous vineyards further north or east, but the names of William Bihler, John G. Staedler and James G. Fair were big news during a big time for wine.

Staedler appears to have been the first to plant vines in or near Petaluma, in the early 1860s. William Bihler planted vines on the banks of Petaluma creek, on the adjacent hillsides, and in the Lakeville area about 1878. Many vines found their way here in the form of old-world rootstock, smuggled in by Italian, French, German, Swiss and other immigrant European settlers and initially intended for their own "house wine". The mix of grape varieties must have been interesting. The only varieties mentioned in early accounts were Zinfandel and Alicante Bouschet.

Petaluma's first winery was founded in 1884 by G.V. Fischer. He took over an abandoned brewery to handle his first crush. There were also two wineries in the Lakeville area at that time. The largest was owned by James G. Fair — a U.S. Senator from Nevada, a famous silver baron, and the man who built the Fairmont Hotel in San Francisco. Fair's winery was located in General Vallejo's old brick armory on Lakeville Highway, now part of Hendricks Ranch. By 1893, the winery had a 600,000-gallon capacity, making it one of the largest in the state. The other Lakeville area winery was on the Marcucci Ranch nearby.

By the late 1870s, the French wine industry was facing near-extinction. An infestation of a root-borne aphid called "phylloxera" was

Petaluma's first winery was founded in 1884 by G.V. Fischer.
He took over an abandoned brewery to handle his first crush.
There were also two wineries in the Lakeville area at that time.

killing the vines. There was talk that California might replace France as the major producer of wine. With vineyard land available for $15 to $25 per acre, and the likelihood of making lots of money from growing grapes and producing wine, more and more vines were being planted. In just a decade, vineyard acreage more than quadrupled and the number of wineries did the same. The "Wine Rush" was on!

In the early 1900s, in the Petaluma area alone, there were at least 1,000 acres of grape vines. Then came the dark ages of Prohibition and our own battle with "phylloxera" here in the North Bay. The aphid, it seems, had now developed a taste for California vines, especially when they were planted on the wrong rootstock. By the time Prohibition ended, what had been a rapidly growing industry was reduced to near wreckage. James Fair had purchased the Bihler vineyards in 1891, but he died in1894. His sons sold what remained. Only one vineyard planted before the turn of the century, owned by the Marcuccis, survived until 1965.

But that was the past — and slowly the vines have crept back, often taking the place of cattle, sheep and chickens in our area's agricultural economy. Most plantings that have propelled the Petaluma Gap wines to their current levels of fame have taken place since the early 1990s.

WHEREFORE THE PETALUMA GAP?

Like the rings of an onion, the Petaluma Gap is situated in an appellation within an appellation within yet another appellation. The largest appellation — or American Viticultural Area (AVA) — surrounding the Petaluma Gap is the California North Coast AVA. It includes Napa, Sonoma, Mendocino and Lake Counties, plus portions of Marin and Solano Counties — including roughly half the total number of wineries in the state. Within the California North Coast AVA lies the Sonoma County AVA. Sonoma County was once part of an inland sea until plate tectonics pushed up the coastal ranges. Volcanic Mount St. Helena contributed ash and red volcanic soils, while the meandering Russian River left alluvial deposits, giving Sonoma County a veritable patchwork of different soils. The coastal mountains, hills, valleys and river benchland created micro-climates that made growing almost any varietal of grape possible somewhere in the county.

Narrowing the focus further, we come to the smaller Sonoma Coast AVA that gives its name to the wines produced in the Petaluma Gap. "Sonoma Coast" is the largest single AVA in Sonoma County, sprawling from Mendocino County in the north to San Pablo Bay in the south, and from Napa County in the east to the Pacific Ocean in the west. The Sonoma Coast AVA encompasses almost a half million acres of land. Only about 7,000 acres are planted in vines, however — less than 1.4% of its total area. On the southernmost boundary of the Sonoma Coast AVA lies the Petaluma Gap, one of the most challenging and intriguing areas in which to grow vines.

IN SHARP FOCUS

Geographically, the Petaluma Gap borders West Marin and Valley Ford on the west, then follows Chileno Valley and Spring Hill Roads to Adobe Road on the east, Cotati on the north and Lakeville Highway on the southeast. This is not your normal geography. As inland valley air heats up, it pulls the cool coastal air into a naturally formed 15-mile-wide "gap" in the coastal range mountains. The wind flows off the ocean between Tomales and Bodega Bay, cuts across the "gap," and empties into San Francisco Bay. Wind and fog define the area, giving the term "micro-climate" real meaning.

Of course, it's not just the Petaluma Gap that benefits. The Pacific breezes and fog work their way inland, cooling not just the immediate Gap area, but also influencing three neighboring AVAs. Contrary to popular opinion, more of the wind and coolness that makes the Carneros AVA so challenging comes from the Petaluma Gap than from San Pablo Bay. Even farther to the northeast, the winds and fog push inland to the Bennett Valley and continue up Sonoma Mountain as well.

The daily weather pattern goes something like this: early- to mid-morning finds a distinctive crisp coolness in the air and likely some dissipating fog. Late morning, the temperature rises and creates the hot part of the day — generally between 11 a.m. and 1 p.m. Then come the cool breezes, flowing west to east, picking up speed as the afternoon progresses, and turning into winds that bring in the almost nightly fog. There are daily temperature swings of forty to fifty degrees, and the cooling "wind tunnel" effect means the yields are smaller and the grapes ripen later, developing wonderful flavors and fruit characteristics, while maintaining ideal levels of acidity. It's the perfect recipe for delicious, well-balanced wines.

Geographically, the Petaluma Gap borders West Marin and Valley Ford on the west,
then follows Chileno Valley and Spring Hill Roads to Adobe Road on the east,
Cotati on the north and Lakeville Highway on the southeast.

There is something wonderful, almost magical, about vineyards. Acres of tidy rows with their canopy of green cover hillsides and valleys, some marching east to west, others north to south. In the Petaluma Gap, the vineyards are widespread but they are on the leading edge of more to come.

The unusual climate that so challenges growers also helps create near-perfect growing conditions for specific varietals. The grape varieties that grow best here and produce the most exceptional wines are Pinot Noir and Chardonnay. Another variety that has done exceptionally well here is Syrah, and it's made into some of the best wine the variety can produce. Since it's a very versatile grape, you'll find Syrahs planted in very warm climates as well — but the cool weather Syrahs seem to explode with fresh fruit and flavor while maintaining an ideal balance of soft acidity and tannins.

It was once thought that the cooling effect of the fog on the Petaluma Gap was too extreme to allow the grapes to ripen fully enough to create high quality premium wines. Don't tell that to the nearly four dozen grape growers and wineries who are producing about 30,000 cases of wine annually.

HARVEST TIME

ALAN PLISSKIN

WINES, VINES AND RECOGNITION

The wines and wineries of the Petaluma Gap fairly exploded on the California wine scene just a year ago, sending the wine media into a frenzy and adding a new name to the California wine landscape. "They popped" — as one local wine merchant put it — winning Gold and Double Gold medals and points ratings up there in the stratosphere. They became the newest "darlings" of the California wine world. Fine restaurants are clamoring for them. The likes of Cyrus, John Ash and the Ritz-Carlton in San Francisco are pouring Petaluma Gap wines. Top wine shops try to score a few cases for their best customers. They're "hot" — the latest, greatest, "happening" thing!

Then there are the wineries themselves, almost twenty as of this writing. Some are amazingly small, but growing, and their numbers are increasing as more and more grape growers realize the joys and rewards of making, bottling and marketing their own wines. Early in the wine business, wines and grapes were connected to names. Now

the names are connected to wineries. Among the growing number of labels to look for are Keller Estates, Copeland Creek, Herrerias Cellars, Ridgeway Family Vineyards, Volamus Vineyards, Adobe Road Winery, Griffin's Lair Vineyards, Armagh Vineyard, Kastania Vineyards, Clary Ranch, Sutton Cellars, Windy Hill Winery, Sonoma Valley Portworks, and the newly completed Azari Winery. The number of wineries in the Petaluma Gap is ever-changing and elusive, though. By the time you read this, more should be added to the list.

Many of the Petaluma Gap growers sell their grapes to larger wineries such as Bouchaine, Landmark, Lost Canyon and Cline Cellars. If you'd like to see a committed display of confidence for the future, no less a winery than Rodney Strong Vineyards has planted Chardonnay vines along Lakeville Highway. It's an exciting and dynamic time for Petaluma Gap wines.

LIFE'S LITTLE PLEASURES...

Amongst the vines you might find a sign indicating a runway is nearby or horse stables. You might even find a road that is occasionally converted into a small racetrack. And, of course, there is the ever-present interest in cars that winery owners and growers often share — old cars or very, very fast ones.

A search for vineyards will take you into the most unexpected places. You might drive into a modest looking housing development and find backyard vines planted behind houses. Some "backyards" — like Timo Rivetti's — just happen to be on a hillside, and his chosen "landscaping" happens to be grape vines. He just "happens" to make a rather excellent Syrah — family hand-harvested, pressed, fermented, aged (yes, in barrels), and bottled, all in a garage and a shed "out back." Rivetti is what is called a "garagiste" — a French word that refers to renegade winemakers in Bordeaux who decided they wanted to make wine using methods outside the traditional mainstream. Here, the meaning of the term is similar — but with a slight twist — referring to out-of-the-mainstream winemakers who make wines in their garages, houses and sheds. Rivetti's latest triumphs have earned him a Double Gold Medal and Best of Class for his "Que Syrah Syrah" label. He produces a mere 37 cases from a half-acre vineyard.

When looking for vines, there are the special little surprises that make you stop in your tracks, staring in absolute wide-eyed wonder at what you see. Drive up a hillside to Keller Estate and you'll understand.

©Marie Lynne

MARIE LYNNE

The Petaluma Gap is not an area of wall-to-wall grape vines, and therein lies the charm and the adventure in searching for them. The individual vineyards and wineries also serve various and diverse passions, so there are amazing little pleasures and surprises everywhere.

SAMANTHA GRAF

You'll need an appointment to visit, but, here, the wines are just part of the immense pleasure.

If you're into horses, history, wetlands, swans and vineyards, there's Rockin' H Ranch and Hendricks Vineyard. If you catch Gary Hendricks in, he just might take you down to see the swans and regale you with stories of General Vallejo's armory, turned wine cellar and storage. It has been preserved as part of Hendrick's house.

If you thrill to spectacular racing cars as well as Double Gold Medal wines, there's Adobe Road Winery, owned by sports car racer and entrepreneur Kevin Buckler and his wife, Debra. The tasting room is open to the public on a limited basis, and approaching it through the racing cars is a thrill in itself.

Then there's Kastania Vineyards. Its owners Hoot and Linda Smith are warm and welcoming. You'll need an appointment to visit, but you'll want to stay, sample some of their celebrated wines, and maybe even volunteer to help. It's that comfortable.

Among many small gems of wines and vineyards are those that don't have tasting rooms. Copeland Creek Vineyard winemaker, Don Baumhefner, does frequent tastings of his exceptionally rated wines at Della Fattoria in downtown Petaluma.

Here's an interesting option: You can now buy a beautiful home in an exclusive housing development, with 40 acres of land and selected rooms constructed to allow for a small winemaking facility and cellar.

In fact, planting a vineyard is a requirement for purchasing. Vineyard management services are available to make the job easier. You can make and bottle all or part of your own wines or sell your grapes to a larger producer. Ron Herrerias came up with the concept. Until recently, he was a grower — the owner of Adobe Road Vineyard. He sold it to pursue his dream of becoming a first class wine-maker — and he has succeeded.

The wines of the Petaluma Gap are amazing, but most impressive of all are the people themselves, the growers and winemakers — some of the nicest people you could ever hope to raise a glass with. They are real and down-to-earth, extremely committed, and willing to share their knowledge, hopes and dreams. It is absolutely clear that they are passionate about what they are doing and where they are going — and that's nowhere but up.

THE FUTURE STARTS NOW

Realizing their uniqueness, a coalition of growers, winemakers and wineries formed the Petaluma Gap Grape and Wine Alliance in 2006. From small producers like Timo Rivetti — who makes only about 3 dozen cases a year — to the Keller Estate which makes thousands of cases, this group came together with the goals of sharing resources, helping and supporting one another's premium winemaking efforts, sharing the rewards and successes, and putting the rest of the California winemaking areas on notice that the Petaluma Gap has arrived. It will never again be the quiet little footnote in the California wine world that it once was.

What about the future? Only 500 acres are now planted to vines, but more will surely follow. Does the Petaluma Gap have the distinguishable geographic, climatic and historic features to warrant awarding its growers a new AVA designation? You bet! The benefit of establishing their own AVA would be to highlight the unique identity of the Petaluma Gap — tied to the on-the-edge climate that makes for such sensational wines. Perhaps, in years to come, there will be a Petaluma Gap AVA. For now, most growers and wineries seem content to produce and market their wines under the excellent laurels of the Sonoma Coast AVA — and to enjoy their position as the newest star in the Sonoma County wine world.

SIXTEEN

PETALUMA CELEBRATES
by Terry Smith

Petaluma is a town
that loves to celebrate.

OFFICIAL PAINTING FOR ART IN THE PARK 2007 BY LORI CHATTERTON

Petaluma is a town that loves to celebrate. Fortunately, there are many opportunities.

Almost every month of the year, there's at least one good excuse for a parade or a party — commemorating our history, our artistic and culinary creativity, or our community spirit. On the following pages, you'll find a month-by-month calendar of the biggest and best of them.

Petaluma's Celebration calendar

logically begins in April, with Butter & Egg Days. The foundation for the modern parade was laid by Herbert Kerrigan, Petaluma's version of P. T. Barnum. Kerrigan staged the first National Egg Day in 1918, complete with a parade down Main Street and an Egg Queen. The parade included a 10-foot-high, 15-foot-long egg basket. A few years later, a giant chicken was added to the basket.

Kerrigan's early celebrations drew national attention — and even Hollywood newsreel cameras. Just over a decade later, however, Kerrigan moved on — after running well over budget on his proposed fairgrounds repairs — and the National Egg Day parades disappeared with him.

The idea for the modern Butter & Egg Days parade was hatched by Linda Buffo and Alice Forsyth in 1981. Forsyth was then Director of the Downtown Merchants Association and Buffo was an active member. They were searching for a springtime event to stimulate business downtown and, in a Mickey Rooney moment, decided, "Let's put on a parade!" The last Saturday in April was chosen, and the event has grown almost every year for nearly three decades. In 2007, the parade was the largest in its 26-year history — with 160 entries and 30,000 spectators lining the sidewalks.

Instead of an Egg Queen, we now choose a "Good Egg" and "Petaluma's Cutest Chick." Both Buffo and Forsyth have been honored

CLO RIDES A FIRE ENGINE IN THE 2007 BUTTER & EGG PARADE HONORING THE 150TH ANNIVERSARY OF THE PETALUMA FIRE DEPARTMENT.

TERRY SMITH

as "Good Eggs" for their "eggs-ceptional" efforts to preserve and promote Petaluma and its history.

The Butter & Egg Days parade is a true hometown celebration. It often seems that half our population is in the parade and half is on the curb watching. Bill Rhodes may have described it best: "It's like a ribbon of love wrapping itself around the town."

Petaluma celebrates History Week with dozens of events during the week preceding the Butter & Egg Days Parade. The Sunday after the parade, the Spring Antique Faire hosts more than 180 dealers along Fourth and Kentucky Streets — and draws more than 10,000 visitors. That same afternoon, restaurants, organizations, and individuals compete at the Great Petaluma Chili Cookoff to raise money for Cinnabar Theater's Youth Programs.

Also in April, the Petaluma Area Chamber of Commerce presents Community Awards to deserving citizens at a gala banquet, and Petaluma hosts the District Three Dairy Princess Ball.

LEFT: SWEEPSTAKES-WINNING FLOAT IN THE 2006 BUTTER & EGG DAYS PARADE HONORING THE CENTENNIAL OF THE CARNEGIE LIBRARY

BOTTOM LEFT: CUTEST LITTLE CHICK IN THE 2005 BUTTER & EGG DAYS PARADE

BOTTOM RIGHT: THE PETALUMA YACHT CLUB KAZOO MARCHING BAND IN THE 2007 BUTTER & EGG DAYS PARADE

TERRY SMITH

SALUTE TO *AMERICAN GRAFFITI*

COURTESY PETALUMA RIVER CLEAN-UP COMMITTEE

RIVER CLEAN-UP IS A FAMILY AFFAIR

In the month of May every year, residents and visitors go "Through the Garden Gate" to view some of Petaluma's most beautiful private gardens — and the proceeds benefit the Petaluma Historical Museum. Scores more volunteer for the River Clean-Up — a day of clearing trash from the waters and banks of the Petaluma River. Of course, the Clean-Up is followed by a barbeque and party.

May is also the month when more than 75 area artists participate in the "Spirit of Color" show and sale. The 2007 edition began with a champagne reception. Proceeds benefit arts programs in the schools, as well as programs of the Petaluma People Services Center, the Petaluma Arts Association, and the Petaluma Arts Council.

The biggest event in May, however, is Petaluma's "Salute to *American Graffiti*". The "Salute" is a three-day weekend full of classic car shows, cruises and a street dance — as well as visits by the stars of George Lucas' timeless coming-of-age film, *American Graffiti*. Sponsor Cruisin' the Boulevard, Inc., chooses a different charitable cause to benefit each year. In just two years, "Salute to *American Graffiti*" has become a real crowd-pleaser.

ELWOOD — VOTED WORLD'S
UGLIEST DOG AT THE 2007
SONOMA-MARIN FAIR

The Sonoma-Marin Fair comes to the Petaluma Fairgrounds each June — complete with top-name entertainment; 4H, FFA, arts, crafts, and culinary competitions; midway rides; and, of course, a full complement of "fair food". In recent years, our little fair has drawn the attention of media nationwide with its "Ugliest Dog Contest." In 2007 — the 19th year of the contest — entries came from all over the country. The winner, Elwood, and owner Karen Quigley are from New Jersey. The Associated Press, CNN, and MSNBC trumpeted the news all around the world.

June also sees the beginning of a season of weekly outdoor concerts and Farmer's Markets that continue into the fall.

July's centerpiece

is the Art & Garden Festival. Fourth and Kentucky Streets are lined with exhibits by garden specialists, artists, community organizations, and purveyors of fine food and wine. There's continuous live music for listening or dancing and a "Children's Corner" with activities for kids. All in all, the Art & Garden Festival is a great summer party downtown, celebrating "Petaluma at its Best!"

JIM JOHNSON, STUDIO 7

JIM JOHNSON, STUDIO 7

PETALUMA WATERFRONT
JAZZ FESTIVAL

MUSIC DIRECTOR
PETER WELKER

CAROLE SMITH

TOM CORBETT

AL MOLINA PLAYS AT THE 2006
WATERFRONT JAZZ FESTIVAL

After nearly a decade

at Foundry Wharf, Petaluma Waterfront Jazz blossomed into a full-fledged "festival" in 2006. The expanded event includes bands at multiple venues around the Petaluma River Turning Basin, as well as wine and beer tasting. Attendance is now measured in the thousands, and the Waterfront Jazz Festival has done a great deal to re-introduce Petalumans to the beauty of their riverfront.

In August 2007, the weekend also included quilt displays, competitions and sales throughout the downtown area sponsored by the Petaluma Quilt Guild. In addition, there was an art show along the river and a visit by the Alma, a historic scow schooner that was a workhorse in Petaluma River commerce a century ago.

COURTESY PETALUMA QUILT GUILD

The Petaluma Arts

Association has been presenting its outdoor fine art show and sale, "Art in the Park", for half a century. Each September, Walnut Park is filled for a weekend with exhibits of oil and watercolor paintings, acrylics, pastels, sculpture, photography, pottery, ceramics and more. It's an opportunity to purchase fine art directly from its creators — as well as to enjoy good food and music and participate in raffle drawings for original artworks. Proceeds from "Art in the Park" support arts programs in local schools.

Later in September, an "Artists of Petaluma" juried show with peoples' choice awards is held. Entry fees and a portion of the sales benefit the Petaluma Arts Association and the Petaluma Arts Council.

Petaluma's Fall Antique Faire — also in September — is a reprise of the Spring fair, providing a second chance for antique buffs to browse and buy from the largest selection of dealers gathered in one place anywhere in the Bay Area.

The newest fall celebration is "Taste of Petaluma." Attendees buy tasting tickets good for samples of fine cuisine from Petaluma's finest restaurants, bakeries, and markets. Music and art exhibits add to the festive atmosphere — and the proceeds go to Petaluma's Cinnabar Theater.

FALL ANTIQUE FAIR

EL DIA DE LOS MUERTOS

LA CATRINA BY PETER PEREZ WAS CHOSEN TO APPEAR ON PETALUMA ARTS COUNCIL'S 2007 DAY OF THE DEAD POSTERS, FLYERS AND T-SHIRTS. LA CATRINA IS A TRADITIONAL IMAGE FOR EL DIA DE LOS MUERTOS.

Halloween celebrations in October go well beyond visits to the many area pumpkin patches. Art and music events throughout the downtown area celebrate "El Dia de los Muertos." The Bill Soberanes Halloween Festival at Plaza North remembers the iconic *Argus-Courier* columnist who held annual séances in hopes of connecting with Harry Houdini. Downtown merchants provide a "Trick-or-Treat Trail" for costumed youngsters. The Petaluma Village Premium Outlets hold a "Canine Costume Contest." The Historical Museum leads a tour of Liberty Cemetery and Heritage Homes hosts a Halloween House Tour.

October is also a big month for benefit bashes. The Carousel Fund draws a sell-out crowd with name entertainment, fine food, casino games and an impressive auction. In 2006, Carousel Fund Casino Night raised nearly $180,000 for families with children who are suffering from life-threatening illnesses. Also in October, Petaluma Valley Rotary holds its "Rockin' Oktoberfest" in support of humanitarian and educational projects.

Some sources say

Petaluma's Veterans Day Parade dates back more than eighty years, but the modern history of the parade began with Julius Forcucci. From 1967 until 1983, Forcucci and two WWII buddies walked the parade route together. In 1983, one of Forcucci's friends died and the other was too ill to walk, so Julius marched alone, carrying an American flag. In 1986, he was joined by 50 more veterans, and the annual parade has grown ever since. In 2006, there were more than 60 entries, 750 participants, and a crowd estimated at 5,000. It's considered the largest Veterans Day Parade north of the Golden Gate.

Traditionally, the Petaluma Holiday Season begins on the first Saturday after Thanksgiving, with the slightly unconventional arrival of Santa and Mrs. Claus on the tugboat "Petaluma." Legend has it that Santa and Mrs. Claus have come to the area by tugboat since the time long ago when a thick fog first forced Santa out of the sky and onto the river.

After waving to the crowd gathered on the banks, Santa and his bride debark at the Weller Street docks and somehow manage to personally greet every one of the hundreds of children that press around them as their party moves toward the center of town. Hopes and hugs are shared. Candy is distributed to all. No child who wants to meet Santa is disappointed.

When they reach the Great Petaluma Mill, Santa and Mrs. Claus board their horse-drawn sleigh to lead the colorful Antique Wagon and Horse Procession — a parade of antique stagecoaches and wagons, horse teams, riders in costume and volunteers in Victorian garb that wends its way through Historic Downtown Petaluma.

Petaluma celebrates Christmas

with as much spirit as any other town in America. Businesses and private homes compete for the best lighting displays and post themselves on the "City of Lights Driving Tour" map so residents and visitors alike can enjoy the results. Even boats get into the act, when decorated craft from all around the area participate in the lighted boat parade to the Petaluma River Turning Basin early in December.

Other Christmas celebrations are too many and varied to list — but among them are the benefit Victorian Tea at the Petaluma Museum, Heritage Homes' Holiday Parlour Tour, Hospice of Petaluma's "Light Up a Life" community tree-lighting ceremony, "The Nutcracker" as performed by the Petaluma City Ballet and children from the Petaluma School of Ballet, and holiday art sales, crafts fairs and merchant open houses seemingly without end.

Since Petaluma is blessed with a diverse religious and ethnic population, there are also many holiday festivities revolving around Chanukah, Kwanzaa, and other celebrations.

SCOTT HESS COURTESY PETALUMA VISITORS PROGRAM

TOM CORBETT

SCOTT HESS COURTESY PETALUMA VISITORS PROGRAM

DECORATED PETALUMA HOMES

In January and February, Petalumans celebrate the time-honored customs of welcoming in the New Year and honoring their significant others on Valentine's Day.

Most frequently, these celebrations are held at a restaurant, and it's said that Petaluma has more fine restaurants per capita than any city in the country. That's hard to argue. Traditional favorites continue to flourish and several new establishments open every year.

For those who prefer to celebrate at home, Petaluma's markets provide the finest in locally grown and processed edibles: meats, poultry and eggs, fish and shellfish, artisan dairy products, vegetables and fruits, baked goods — even candies and ice cream. In fact, the availability of high quality ingredients has been a major factor in drawing talented chefs to our town. Petaluma area wineries and microbreweries are recognized as among the best in the nation, too. No matter how we celebrate, we need look no further than the food and drink from our hometown.

LEFT: CINDY CALLAHAN OF BELLWETHER FARMS
TRIGGERED A REVIVAL IN ARTISAN CHEESEMAKING
RIGHT: ST. PAT SPRINGTIME CHEESE FROM COWGIRL
CREAMERY IS WRAPPED IN STINGING NETTLES

MARIN FRENCH CHEESE COMPANY IS THE OLDEST CONTINUOUSLY OPERATING
CHEESE FACTORY IN THE UNITED STATES

Launched in March 2007, the Petaluma Artisan Cheese Festival sponsored by the Sheraton Sonoma County-Petaluma is the newest annual celebration. The four-day festival includes

special dinners, seminars, an artisan cheese marketplace, and opportunities to meet cheese-makers and taste their wares. It even includes visits to nearby farms and cheese-making facilities. The inaugural event drew celebrity chefs and fromagiers, more than 50 artisan cheese producers and related vendors, and more than 1,100 local, out-of-town, and even out-of-state guests. Most events were sold out and sponsors are convinced more space will be needed in 2008.

It was a great beginning for an event designed to celebrate the quality and economic viability of artisan cheese production in our area. Best of all, the event raised $10,000 for non-profit organizations supporting sustainable agriculture: the Marin Agricultural Land Trust, the Sonoma Land Trust, the California Artisan Cheese Guild, the Redwood Empire Food Bank, and the Petaluma Future Farmers of America.

SEVENTEEN

PETALUMA: A CITY ON THE EDGE
by Bruce Hagen

There is cause for health, happiness, and hope — if you show up. It's all here, on the edge, in Petaluma.

Winter Solstice, 1999. The full moon is still hiding behind Sonoma Mountain, but thanks to the irregularities of orbits, she will draw closer to my home than she has in the twenty years since I became a Dad. And the big moon brings with her a big tide. My daughter Laurel and I decide this is time for a hometown adventure, to ride this tide where it might lead.

The sun has dipped below the downtown Petaluma skyline as we lift our canoe from the roof rack and carry it overhead, stiff-armed, down the ramp and into the olive green water of the turning basin. The tide had been pushing salt-scented water up from the Bay. It's still creeping slowly upstream as we begin our journey, paddling quietly under the graceful footbridge.

Right away, the river grants us new perspectives on familiar places: the underbelly of Washington Street; Petaluma's chicken-feed skyscraper reflected in the slack water; a portage over the gas pipe crossing, still bearing flotsam from the last flood.

The "last" flood? We paddle into the City's flood control project, tens of millions of dollars ploughed into the promise of winning the fight against wild rain, wind, and tide — and against the wild abandon of industrial civilization and its self-inflicted weaknesses. We move between mountains of earth heaved against the corrugated green iron floodwall — the last line of defense against the next big one. Washington Creek comes in from the east, and then Lynch Creek, spilling down its concrete terminus cascade. Both streams bisect

flatland Petaluma, and stretch all the way back to the upper flanks of Sonoma Mountain. We pause, floating in this focal point of the Petaluma River watershed. It's calm, as though before a storm.

Just above the confluence with Lynch is the floodgate: a huge, notched concrete wall spanning the man-made channel. Exactly six years and ten days later this floodgate wall would become a check dam, fulfilling its mission to protect those homes on the Payran floodplain downstream. But upstream, alas! Land once considered safe went under. The Petaluma Village Premium Outlets, Auto Row, and businesses seemingly a safe distance back from the flood plain were hit. The damages, estimated at $55 million, were close to twice the cost of the flood control project. One must wonder, are we doomed to a never-ending game of hydraulic whack-a-mole, where one neighborhood's gain is another one's loss?

The floodgate marks the upper end of the project. It is also a boundary between worlds. As we glide through, iron and concrete become oak and willow. Cars and barking dogs give way to egrets and honking ducks. Laurel and I soon lose track of our precise whereabouts.

We are happily lost in riparian deep space until we find ourselves passing under the old railroad trestle, portal to a canyon of cascading blackberry vines. More leisurely paddling, some wet-shoe bushwacking, and we reach the end, the tip of this groping finger of the Pacific. Beaching our canoe, we climb up the bank and…revelation! We have popped through a wormhole, out of Nature and into the parking lot of the Outlet Mall. Thankyougoodbye!

We retreat to the riverine canopy. The sun sets, the tide turns, and we follow the current home in twilight stillness. Back through the ancient oak-willow world, through the gray gate, into the modern flood wall world. Back with a radically new perspective.

We look at the hundreds of homes and businesses built in the river's path, and wonder: what were they *thinking*, those who put them so close to harm? Myopic ignorance, cynical greed? Who's to say? That was half a century ago. We know better now, don't we? Today we have a flood wall and (sometimes) a City Council to protect us from the water racing downstream. But what are we doing to protect us tomorrow from the floods coming *upstream*, catching Petaluma in a pincer?

For it was the ocean that carried our canoe so far north; the same ocean that will lift up to greet the rising levels of greenhouse gases in the atmosphere. At the close of the second millennium, when Laurel and I took this trip, denial of the climate crisis was still the norm. Much has changed since then. There is real progress, real hope. But we since have learned ocean level increases of two feet during Laurel's lifetime are the "best case" scenario. What will *that* cost our fair city?

Petaluma lies on the edge of earth's one ocean. If that ocean rises up against human foolishness, we will suffer directly. "The climate is a capricious beast, and we are poking it with a sharp stick," wrote Wally Broeker, a prominent climate scientist. Peel away the denial and you expose gut-level dread. Catastrophic hundred year floods — one hundred million dollar floods — will become regular visitors, as will protracted droughts, killing not just our lawns but our oak woodlands, our dairy farms. Many years ago, I started composing a lyric for a song about my children that I found too sad to continue writing: "The greatest fear / I have found: / that I might leave you in this world / before we turn this world around." My youngest son now approaches twenty, and we talk around the edges of what the future holds. He's bright, web-savvy, and knows what's going on in the world. How do I give him, or any of our children, hope?

I tell him: it's still a secret to many, but we live in a city on the edge of the ocean. We live on the edge of disaster and of redemption, of profound horror and profound beauty. We live here as part of a civilization and a city, and as citizens. Maybe it seems impossible to change even this city, much less our civilization, but they are no more than the sum of what each citizen contributes, for good or ill. And you, my children, decide. You decide how you will live. If you live simply, taking little and giving much, you will be more able to personally weather any storm. And you will be helping to calm the storm before it strikes.

What to do is no secret any more. Pursue enlightenment though the spiritual discipline of your choice. That's the foundation, the enabler, that from which other good things will flow. Follow the golden rule. Shrink your ecological footprint as you shrink your self-will, and with loving kindness, help others along the path.

I would tell them: you won't find a better place to walk this path than Petaluma, a City whose slogan ought to be "We Show Up." When there are crises great or small, or just everyday opportunities to care for each other, we are there. When real estate developers were poised to bankrupt the City with unchecked sprawl, Petaluma showed up in the Supreme Court to establish the public's right to limit growth. When Polly Klaas disappeared, we showed up everywhere in search. We show up at events to help the homeless, to plant community gardens, to take back parks and paths from vandals, drug dealers, and sociopaths. We turn out to fund our schools and open space. We show up at City Hall to demand a healthy and sustainable community.

Petaluma has the resources, human and natural, to support this transformation for citizens, city, and civilization. Besides a large variety of traditional and not-so-traditional churches, we have nearby the Blue Mountain and Spirit Rock meditation centers. There are many innovative public, charter, and private centers of learning, including New College and The Institute for Noetic Studies. There are nearly unlimited opportunities for volunteer community service. The City, many businesses, and a variety of non-profit groups are practicing and promoting green living. And our resources are growing with each passing day.

There is cause for health, happiness, and hope — if you show up. It's all here, on the edge, in Petaluma.

EIGHTEEN

PICTURING PETALUMA'S FUTURE
by Connie Madden

"Everything Old
is New Again!"

song by Peter Allen from the musical "All That Jazz"

"CLOUDY BEND"

In my mind's eye, I am picturing a bright day in 2028. A Cessna Skyhawk rises from Petaluma Airport, transporting a tourist couple into the blue sky above this picturesque river town.

As they fly south, the pilot provides historic and scenic highlights. From the air, green spaces abound. Once known as the World's Egg Basket and for hosting the World Wrist-Wrestling Championship, Petaluma was also the first town in America with a Supreme Court-approved plan for controlling residential growth. At the turn of the 21st century, Petaluma's Parks Department could boast 40 parks covering 325 acres — with seven miles of landscaped medians, bike trails, open space areas, two swim centers, a Community Center, a Teen Center, a Senior Center, a marina with 190 slips, and the Petaluma Historic Library and Museum. Programs included leisure classes, specialty camps, aquatic classes, technology workshops for children, fencing, tennis, engineering, and host of special events including July 4th, Movies in the Park, a Senior Expo, and a Holiday Crafts Faire. In 2028, Petaluma is maintaining its position as a model "Green City" — the Gateway to Wine Country and a hub from which travelers go to the beach, redwoods and all points north.

Wine Country officially begins just south of Petaluma, its county land complementing a sustainable and beautiful urban core. As they fly over vineyards and tasting rooms, the pilot describes Petaluma Gap wines and the micro-climate that produces exceptional Pinot Noir and Chardonnay grapes when evening ocean breezes and mist pour over ripening vines.

As they approach Kastania Road, a herd of Arabian horses moves amid a stand of Valley Oaks creating a pastoral scene. In the wetlands at Shollenberger Park, White Pelicans and little Black Phoebes can be spotted with binoculars, and a family of River Otters cavorts on exercise ramps in the creek.

The pilot checks in with Air Traffic Control to get a go-ahead to drop down over the Petaluma River and show her tourists the historic downtown. McNear Peninsula appears with its small craft rentals along the river, easy walking distance from downtown. The drawbridge rises fully upright as they near it, allowing passage of the paddle wheeler Petaluma Princess, available for charter or occasionally for short river trips on holiday weekends. Many bicycles, walkers, and a few electric scooters and Segways dot the length of the Riverwalk — which stretches all the way to the wetlands and the Audubon Birding Center.

The Petaluma River Turning Basin, seen from above, is bristling with activity, with full tables at outdoor cafes and a fleet of white yachts along the pier. The Petaluma River reflects the blue sky as a flock of white egrets sails past the boats and lands in the creekside redwood trees.

Just beyond the Turning Basin, Petaluma's landmark buildings are stately from above: the Masonic Building with its clock tower, the Carnegie Library and Museum, and the D Street row of fine Victorian homes. The pilot points out several buildings and homes designed by the renowned Victorian-era architect, Brainerd Jones — as well as a few high-tech SMART houses of innovative design.

Flying over the town's central district, the couple exclaims at the expanse of lush trees and water features that mark River Park—with its fishing pond stocked with trout and bass, a man-made lake for swimming and boating and an authentic replica Miwok Teepee on an island reachable over a stone foot bridge. Pedal boats, solar-electric boats and rowboats can be rented for a ride around the lake. Family and company barbeques are frequent at dusk and Tai-Chi practice is offered on most mornings.

The plane flies over River Park's Butterfly and Bug Garden, where children can feed sugar water to Tiger Swallowtail, Monarch and Cabbage butterflies and Petaluma gardeners are given ladybugs and praying mantises to police their home gardens. Next door is the Trailside Museum, housing specimens of native animals, some of which appreciate being petted by visiting children. Trailside staff members are aided by many high school volunteers.

River Park is a favorite with Petaluma families, but also draws visitors from around the entire region. Admission is free for locals and inexpensive for out-of-towners. There's an ornate antique replica merry-go-round, and there are hiking trails, campgrounds and organic fast food vendors. Soccer and baseball fans find fields here, bocce ball teams have a court, and there is a dog run. A wetlands preserve near the railroad tracks is home to nesting egrets and herons. River Park's future is secured with government and foundation funding for posterity, and volunteer programs help with upkeep. Indeed, sweat equity from the neighbors was a determining factor in the creation of River Park, which involved considerable digging, hauling, planting and landscaping.

The plane turns toward Sonoma Mountain, viewing the Lafferty Ranch hiking trails, creek and small waterfall from above. A Sonoma Mountain Trail begins at Lafferty and winds all the way to Jack London State Park, a favorite campground with wildflowers, high vistas and access to Adobe Creek. Turning back from the hills, the plane passes over an expanded Santa Rosa Junior College and Eastside Swimming Pool, filled with children.

Landing, the passengers find they have dozens of restaurants to choose from for dinner — including Italian, Thai, Greek, Mexican, French and Sonoma County cuisine. Most feature the locally grown organic foods for which the area has become known.

They have booked a room at a downtown hotel, busy with tourists and convention-goers headed for Bill Soberanes Civic Center on the fairgrounds. After a pleasant night, the couple explores Petaluma on foot and on Borrow Bikes signed out at the Transit Hub. They ride past murals, fountains, and sculptures that are the result of the community's dedication to civic art. Stopping at the Visitors Center, the couple learns that public funds also support a lecture series, theater and dance programs. The music and arts scenes continue to blossom as well.

The afternoon is given over to shopping and gathering souvenirs in Petaluma's Historic Downtown. The couple strolls Kentucky Street, Petaluma Boulevard, Western Avenue and Theater Square, finding gifts for family and friends, stylish and affordable clothes, and an amazing array of toys and museum-quality antiques. That evening they leave Petaluma with good memories and a wish to return soon.

NURTURING THE GOOD LIFE ALONG THE WATER

Petaluma in 2028 retains the hometown character we celebrated in our Sesquicentennial year. The town's traditional annual events — Butter & Egg Days, Santa's Riverboat Arrival, the Holiday Lighted Boat Parade, the Veteran's Day Parade, the Art & Garden Show, the Great Petaluma Chili Cook-off, Taste of Petaluma, spring and fall Antique Faires, salute to *American Graffiti*, and so many more — continue to grow, making Petaluma more and more a vacation destination every year.

The Transit Hub at the Depot is true to its name, providing transportation for both passengers and freight to destinations such as Petaluma and Sonoma Airports, Armstrong Redwoods, Point Reyes, Healdsburg, Sonoma and Napa. To the south, Golden Gate Transit buses and SMART trains take travelers and commuters to Marin and San Francisco and to ferries reaching San Francisco, Tiburon and Vallejo. Tickets are available through the Visitors Center for Dolphin and American Safari cruises, including waterborne Wine Country tours.

Young people are well served in the Petaluma of 2028 I envision. Though budding gang activity and vandalism worried residents early in the century, by 2028 most teens are engaged, entertained and connected. The Boys and Girls Club is going strong and Mentor Me Petaluma has tripled in size, offering one-on-one mentoring for nearly every child in need. Through school and community programs Petaluma youth are helping harvest crops in community gardens, assisting at the Senior Center, serving in high school cafeterias, and helping rebuild and refurbish homes and public buildings. Sports, music and arts programs are plentiful and every high school senior is expected to attend a meeting of the City Council and make a brief public comment. Schools require preventive health care courses and basic health and dental care is available for everyone.

GENERAL PLAN 2045

After long public deliberation and debate, the City Council in 2028 is expected to adopt its General Plan 2045 — reaffirming our Urban Growth Boundary, committing to SMART Codes and environmental innovation, and working toward a healthy economy and lifestyle for residents. Land use changes for GP 2045 include additional density downtown, more mixed use commercial and rental buildings, more low-income and workforce housing and a plan to provide every neighborhood with a neighborhood center, a walkable community core, and bicycle lanes to downtown.

Economic stability has been aided by use of Community Impact Reports (CIRs). CIRs provide understanding of long-term local economic health with results indicating the mix of stores and services that would best serve the population. Through the offices of a Business Ombudsman, the city is courting desirable new businesses and guiding them through the permit process.

Based on the citizenry's historic support of environmental programs, the City Council has committed to a 90% reduction in greenhouse gas emissions by 2038. Police and fire fleets will be replaced with plug-in vehicles. Tax credits will go to homeowners and renters using wind and solar units, plug-in cars and energy efficient appliances. Most Petalumans are learning to do much more with "off the grid" energy sources — using solar ovens for small baking jobs, growing some of their own food, and recycling more and more consumer goods. Some have even rigged exercycles to generate a portion of their household energy needs, and many have solar panels or wind turbines.

To ensure water availability, rainwater catchment and conservation have become part of our Municipal Code in 2028. Many cisterns have been built. Reverse osmosis for grey water is becoming affordable, creating a new source of drinking water as well as water for golf courses, lawns, agriculture and sanitation.

By 2028, home permaculture gardens on porches, and trained up walls, are allowing residents to reduce their "ecological footprints" — reducing car trips and shipping costs. A goal of 50% locally grown has proven achievable by 2028, and a new goal of 80% has been set for 2045. We have learned to live more within our means — sharing recipes that feature the produce we grow ourselves and growing extra tomatoes, beans and cherries to freeze or sun dry, vacuum pack, and can for use off-season. All these activities are saving money and bringing families and friends closer together.

This Petaluma of the future boasts a world-class Petaluma Center for Well-Being, a full-service medical center with a special focus on preventive medicine. The Center rewards doctors for supporting healthy habits. While some elective procedures require health insurance, no one is denied basic health care.

The Center uses biochemical, genetic and psychological testing to provide each patient with an individualized health regimen. The regimen is based on traditional Western medical models, state-of-the-art lab testing, and biogerontology work-ups (the study of aging) — but alternative medical practices such as Ayurvedic and Chinese medicine are also available. Petaluma residents can attend meditation or yoga classes or lectures, and get herbal referrals, biofeedback, massage, nutritional consultation and acupuncture with trained family counselors. With its sauna, steam room and mineral baths, the Center has also become popular with tourists, providing some of the financial support for its medical facilities.

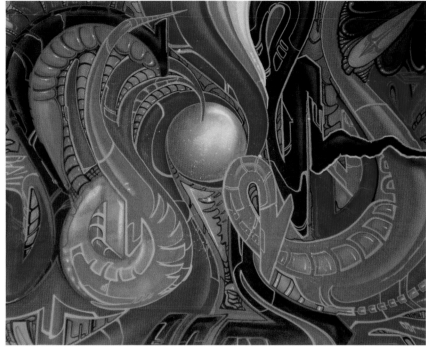

"MERGENCE OF MAN AND MACHINE" BY RICKY WATTS

The wisdom and skills of our senior citizens have found new applications through consultative services and the highly valued volunteer projects that thrive in Petaluma. Seniors are helping in the schools as if they were an extended family. The village of Petaluma has truly become a "healthy community" for all ages and ethnicities. Ethnic diversity is acknowledged to be an asset to the community and diverse cultures, foods and traditions are celebrated.

2058: PETALUMA'S BICENTENNIAL CELEBRATIONS ARE UNDERWAY!

What do I see life being like in Petaluma's Bicentennial year? Will there be computerized cars in the air and on land offering hands-free driving and reducing traffic fatalities? Will Sky cars, similar to those seen in *The Fifth Element*, fill the air above the city and along transportation corridors — allowing people to hop aboard anytime and eliminating the need to own automobiles? Will homes be energy-saving condos or apartments with shared community rooms — both more affordable and more sociable than single-family dwellings?

Technology will likely be everywhere and mostly invisible. Basic services and products might be purchased with a scan of a thumb.

Imperceptible to the human eye, nanobots may be helping us save lives and money. By 2058, tiny robotic particles will likely be valuable in health care, manufacturing, and many other fields. Genetic engineering, cloning and robotics may make Petaluma singer-songwriter Larry Potts' song, "Full Body Transplant," an actual possibility.

I foresee Petaluma becoming a hub for new technology. I see innovative companies inhabiting its business parks, creating products we can't even imagine today. By the time our Bicentennial year arrives, I can see caring, resourceful Petalumans actively involved in meeting challenges that have arisen in the environment, healthcare, housing, transportation and more. Yet, I believe that Petaluma's historic landscape will remain familiar. I believe that, as much as Petaluma has to offer in the future, it will continue to honor and learn from its past.

NINETEEN

PROUD TO CALL PETALUMA HOME
by David Glass, Mayor of Petaluma 2003–2006

I will never forget our most recent flooding disaster — on New Year's Eve morning, December 31, 2005.

Petaluma is a unique

and wonderful town. Variously known as the "Egg Basket of the World", the home of the World Wrist-Wrestling Championships, and the location where the classic motion picture *American Graffiti* was filmed — Petaluma is recognized throughout the United States. Our historic downtown is a cherished reminder of the charm of the past. Our river is treasured or cursed depending upon the season: we come together to enjoy River Festivals with the sound of great jazz under the direction of Peter Welker in the summertime, and we have been known to come together to battle the river's waters as they crest its banks in the wintertime.

I will never forget our most recent flooding disaster — on New Year's Eve morning, December 31, 2005. Our community center had been opened in the middle of the night to provide shelter for those evacuated from their homes as the rain mercilessly pounded our city. The tides were rising and the danger was increasing when a call came in notifying command control that a boat was about to break loose in the turning basin. If it were to become a runaway, it could crash, break apart, and create a dam holding water back from getting downstream — greatly increasing the already rising water levels in Petaluma. This was a time for action. Members of our fire department, along with local volunteer Chris Lind, were asked to secure the boat. It was dark, wet and slippery, and there were clearly personal risks. Nevertheless, within 15 minutes the job was done, and the town was spared a potentially much more severe loss of property and perhaps life. City staff in every department worked around the clock that night removing people and property from harm's way. The Red Cross answered the call as well. As I traveled Petaluma that night, talking to those who had been

displaced, I was awed by the cooperation and efficiency I witnessed. While there was 56 million dollars in property damage, there were no injuries or deaths. In large part, that was because of the willingness of so many citizens to do what had to be done.

This "can do" and "will do" spirit does not come as a surprise to anyone who has been around Petaluma for a while. Several years ago, the City was in the early stages of the revitalization of downtown Petaluma. The School District was in danger of losing its shop program. This very valuable curriculum trains students in work skills that will enable them to earn a living for a lifetime. A plan was proposed in which the City of Petaluma, Petaluma High School and local trade unions would work together to produce furniture for the downtown area. It was produced with precision and quality — on time, and under budget. The business class put together a business plan, the architecture class designed the product, and the shop classes produced it. All gained valuable experience in the process. The teachers most responsible for the success of this program were Tom Richards and

Dan Sunia — both of whom worked many hours above and beyond the call of duty to ensure its success. The accomplishments of Mr. Sunia recently led to statewide recognition.

Petaluma is also unique in that it is home to more non-profit organizations than any other city its size in the United States.

COTS provides shelter for the homeless. In order to receive help, homeless people must adhere to strict rules and demonstrate real effort towards becoming productive citizens. In my mind, that is why COTS programs are so well received and supported by the community. COTS is about a hand up rather than a handout.

The DARE program is a partnership between our police department, the city schools, and local volunteers. One of the most powerful programs they present is "Every Fifteen Minutes" — a dramatic production which illustrates what happens somewhere in our country every 15 minutes as the result of the mixture of drinking and driving. It shows how a fatal automobile accident can have many victims beyond those directly involved.

The McDowell Drug Task Force is in its third decade of work in Petaluma. It educates our kids about the dangers of drugs, alcohol, and drinking and driving. Dick Sharke has worked thousands of volunteer hours and has provided the inspiration for this vitally needed program.

Petaluma People Services Center provides meals on wheels for senior shut-ins, renters assistance programs for those in need, door-to-door transportation services with wheelchair accessibility, employment and counseling services and many other programs which meet PPSC's mission statement of improving the social and economic health of our community. Many of our citizens volunteer their time through PPSC.

Some towns are lucky to have one Boys and Girls Club. We have eight locations, conveniently located all over town, ensuring that our kids have a place to both study and play.

The Petaluma Educational Foundation has provided thousands of scholarships through the years, as well as grants to our local schools. This year, the total scholarship money given by PEF was more than one million dollars.

Our local service clubs such as the Rotary, Lions, and Kiwanis are always available to pitch in and do whatever needs to be done, wherever it needs to be done.

The Lions Club, for instance, supports Project Graduation with a fundraising dinner. Virtually every restaurant in town provides food and local wineries provide wine for one of the most enjoyable evenings anywhere. If you haven't attended this event, you have missed something special — and the money supports an all-night party on graduation night for our seniors. They enjoy it, they win prizes and, most important to all of us, they stay safe.

The business community rallies to the needs of Petaluma through the Chamber of Commerce. Each year dedicated members of their Leadership Class identify ways to better our community. In addition, local citizens volunteer their hours and ideas to the Petaluma Visitors Program, helping make our community more attractive to visitors.

Individual businesses, too, seem always willing to step up to the plate. Several years ago we were in danger of having to cancel the 4th of July Fireworks show. However, Basin Street Properties and Shamrock Materials donated the money needed and, as a result, the tradition of a free fireworks show continues to this day.

The Carousel Fund organized by Arnie Cohen has raised many thousands of dollars to help families with children suffering from life threatening illnesses. Each year for the past two decades, Petalumans attending the Carousel Fund's October gala have provided about $170,000 in relief to families whose medical bills are rising steeply even as they find they must spend more and more time away from their jobs.

The Superb 7 is a group of seven teenage girls who worked tirelessly and with great passion advocating for a downtown movie theater. They drafted a business plan, attended countless meetings, and never lost the faith that their advocacy and hard work would pay off. Now seven stars with the girls' names on them are set in the sidewalk outside the Boulevard Cinemas, a theater complex that anchors a great gathering spot for young and old in Petaluma.

Witness, too, the generosity of Johnny Gomes — a native Petaluman who made it to baseball's major leagues with the Tampa Bay Devil Rays. Gomes now sponsors three Little League teams in Petaluma, and his fans show their appreciation by showing up by the hundreds when the Devil Rays visit Oakland.

The examples above only begin to describe the generosity of spirit of the citizens of Petaluma. There are so many organizations that selflessly provide help to people in need in Petaluma and around the world — and so many stories of individual kindness and sharing — that this book could never contain them all. I guess that's the point, and that is why this is a town I am proud to call home.

NORRIS "BOB" DYER

In 1999, Norris "Bob" Dyer became the first wetlands docent at Shollenberger Park and is currently "Senior Docent" there. His wildlife photographs have appeared in various magazines and on many websites. He also collects stamps and Petaluma chicken memorabilia. Bob and his wife, Brigitte, moved to Petaluma in 1975. Their sons, Kenneth and Timothy, are engineers.

DAVID GLASS

David Glass was elected Mayor of Petaluma in November of 2002 in one of the closest elections in the history of Petaluma — winning by a margin of 78 votes. The former San Francisco Giants radio broadcaster returned to broadcasting after serving his term, hosting a talk show on KSRO radio in Santa Rosa.

BRUCE HAGEN

Bruce Hagen, a 26-year resident of Petaluma, has been writing a bi-weekly column about building sustainable community for the *Petaluma Argus-Courier* since 1998. He loves family, our Earth, Petaluma, writing, music, bicycling, dancing, and too many other things to be itemized here.

MARIANNE HURLEY

Marianne Hurley is an architectural historian and historic preservation specialist with California State Parks. Although based at the district offices near the Petaluma Adobe, her fieldwork includes Sonoma, Marin, Solano, Napa, and Contra Costa counties. She has served on the Historical and Cultural Preservation Committee for five years, and is a contributor to a soon-to-be-published guide to architecture in the San Francisco Bay Area.

VON HURSON

Following an airborne career with Pan Am Airways, Von Hurson's career took off in a new direction: the wine industry. It led her from tasting room staff and events coordinator to wine educator and writer. She is *The Petaluma Post's* wine columnist. She has worked vineyards, made wine, launched a tasting panel for publication and continues her ongoing quest to share her love of all things wine.

CONNIE MADDEN

Connie Madden lives, writes and produces events in Petaluma. She wrote a play, *Trash Planet and the Search for Home* for the United Nations' 60th Anniversary. She writes a Petaluma360.com blog, ConnieMadden.com, and is a frequent contributor to the *Petaluma Argus-Courier* and other publications. She lives in a warehouse sometimes called "The Cave," where she and partner Wayne Morgenthaler share "House Concerts" and an amazing array of other activities they greatly enjoy.

JANET PARMER

Janet Parmer is a writer based in rural Petaluma. She is a contributor to the *Santa Rosa Press Democrat*, and writes for *Napa/Sonoma* magazine. She has also written for *Sunset* and *Parenting* magazines, *The Los Angeles Times*, and *The San Diego Union-Tribune*. She is a former TV news writer and associate producer for KPIX-TV and KQED-TV.

VERN PICCINOTTI

Vernon S. Piccinotti is a fourth generation native of Petaluma who grew up on a family farm in the Two Rock Valley. He graduated from St. Vincent's High School, Petaluma, and the University of San Francisco. He maintains an active interest in Petaluma and Sonoma County history and related projects and is retired from a thirty-five year career in Federal and State law enforcement.

JOANN RITKO POZZI

JoAnn Ritko Pozzi, local Certified Public Accountant, Petaluma native, and past president of Petaluma Area Chamber of Commerce, has been entertaining folks with her snippets of Petaluma oral history. She has presented more than a dozen of these captivating pieces in 2005, 2006 and 2007.

VANGIE PULLINS

Vangie Pullins and husband, Lyndon, own Aurora Colors Gallery and Glass Art Center, an art glass store and studio blended with the latest in fine art. A glass artist, designer, instructor, curator, and a sponsor and volunteer in various Petaluma events, she is president of the Petaluma Arts Association. As a member of the Sesquicentennial Committee, she organized the Youth Art Contest for our 150th Celebration.

BILL RHODES

Bill Rhodes was born and raised in northern California. He served as Chairman of the River Committee, as well as a member of the Executive Board and Board of Directors of the Petaluma Area Chamber of Commerce. He owned PIP Printing for 15 years and was a member of the Board of Directors of the Petaluma Downtown Merchants Association. In 1986, he founded the Petaluma River Festival and was named Petaluma's "Good Egg."

KATHERINE J. RINEHART

Historian Katherine J. Rinehart has been researching and actively advocating for the preservation of Petaluma's historic architecture for over a decade. She currently works for the Sonoma County Library and serves on the board of directors of the Petaluma Museum Association. She is the author of *Petaluma: A History in Architecture* and has her own business specializing in historic research, writing, and lecturing. In 2007, Katherine was named Petaluma's "Good Egg" for her efforts to preserve and promote Petaluma and its history.

GREG SARRIS

Greg Sarris is serving his seventh elected term as Chairman of the Federated Indians of the Graton Rancheria. He is the author of several books, including *Grand Avenue*, which he adapted for an award-winning HBO miniseries.

TERRY SMITH

Terry Smith is Editor and Publisher of *The Petaluma Post*. He is also Chairman of the Petaluma Visitors Program Advisory Board and a member of the Petaluma Sesquicentennial Committee.

BILL SOBERANES

Bill Soberanes was a long-time columnist for both *The Petaluma Argus-Courier* and *The Petaluma Post*. A self-proclaimed "peopleologist", he interviewed — and was photographed with — literally hundreds of international celebrities and local personalities. Soberanes was known as "Mr. Petaluma" because of the endless support he showed for his hometown. Bill Soberanes died on June 2, 2003 — exactly 49 years to the day after writing his first column.

SKIP SOMMER

Skip Sommer is a historian and real estate preservationist. He specializes in the restoration and sale of historic homes and commercial properties. Skip has been responsible for the famed Lark Creek Inn in Larkspur, the River House Restaurant and the Great Petaluma Mill. He is an honorary member of Heritage Homes of Petaluma. He has been the History Editor of *The Petaluma Post* for 20 years. Skip was named Petaluma's "Good Egg" for Butter & Egg Days in 1985.

THE SUPERB SEVEN

When they were still in 7th Grade, seven young women dreamed about bringing the movies back to Petaluma. It took five years, an impressive amount of planning and execution, and an even more impressive amount of courage and persistence, but they succeeded.

Left to right are Liz Comstock, Liza Hall, Taylor Norman, Noelle Bisson, Sarah Marcia, Madison Webb, and Ashley Ditmer.

PAMELA TORLIATT

Pamela Torliatt is a fourth generation Petaluman and has spent the past fifteen years serving the community. From 1992 to 1996 she was a Planning Commissioner. She then spent ten years as a Petaluma City Councilmember. In November 2006, she was elected Petaluma's 19th Mayor.

PETALUMA 150TH CELEBRATION STEERING COMMITTEE

Left to right are Karen Nau, Don Bennett, Theresa Haire, Bill Hammerman, Co-Chair Jessica Vann Gardner, Julie Andersen, Marie McCusker, Lorna Johnson, Terry Smith, Co-Chair Tom Corbett, Jan Mandrell, Thom Butler, Vangie Pullins

Committee members not listed are: Teresa Barrett, Toni Bodenhamer, Deborah Garber, Erica Burns-Gorman, Peg Grubb, Katie Kerns, Karen Langdon, Linda Lipps, Jody Mattei, Karen Phillips, Vern Piccinotti, Katherine Rinehart, Andrea Robertson, Danna Rocca, Esther Schau, Kathy Schmidt, Chris Stevick, Mayor Pamela Torliatt, Marsha Trent, Anne-Marie Woods

FRONT ENDSHEET MAP: Courtesy of the Petaluma Museum Association

BACK ENDSHEET AERIAL MAP: Courtesy of the City of Petaluma, GIS Division; image date April 2006

PUBLISHED BY THE PETALUMA SESQUICENTENNIAL COMMITTEE AND THE PETALUMA VISITORS PROGRAM
© 2007 Petaluma Sesquicentennial Committee and Petaluma Visitors Program
FIRST PRINTING: JANUARY 2008
SECOND EDITION: OCTOBER 2008

INTERNATIONAL STANDARD BOOK NUMBER: 978-0-9801716-0-0

PRINTING: Global Interprint, Santa Rosa, CA - printed in China

EDITOR: Terry Smith

BOOK DESIGN: Nancy Campana, Campana Design, Petaluma, CA

COPY EDITORS: Karen Phillips, Marsha Trent, Tom Corbett, Jessica Vann Gardner, Lorna Johnson, Deborah Garber, Lisle Lee

ART AND PHOTO RESEARCHERS: Norris (Bob) Dyer, Vangie Pullins, Greg Sarris, Tom Corbett, Theresa Haire, Leslie Graebner, Marie McCusker, Susan Villa, Kathy Fries, Marsha Trent, Linda Gonzales